The Way People Live

Life in an Eskimo Village

by Gail B. Stewart

Lucent Books, P.O. Box 289011, San Diego, CA 92198-9011

Titles in The Way People Live Series include:
    Cowboys in the Old West
    Life During the French Revolution
    Life in an Eskimo Village
    Life in the Warsaw Ghetto

To Doug Meeker
for his invaluable insight
into the Yupik culture.

Library of Congress Cataloging-in-Publication Data

Stewart, Gail, 1949–
    Life in an Eskimo village / by Gail B. Stewart.
       p.   cm. — (The Way people live)
    Includes bibliographical references and index.
    ISBN 1-56006-076-X (alk. paper)
    1. Eskimos—Juvenile literature.   [1. Eskimos. 2. Indians of North
America.] I. Title. II. Series.
   E99.E7S827   1995
   973'.04971—dc20   94-16692
                                                         CIP
                                                         AC

Printed in the U.S.A.

Contents

FOREWORD
Discovering the Humanity in Us All   4

INTRODUCTION
"Two Inches Above the Television Screen"   6

CHAPTER ONE
Traditions of the Real People   11

CHAPTER TWO
For the Good of the Community   26

CHAPTER THREE
The Coming of the Outsiders   38

CHAPTER FOUR
"In Their Best Interests"   48

CHAPTER FIVE
Day to Day: Life in the Community   63

CHAPTER SIX
Rough Spots   76

CHAPTER SEVEN
"We Must Make Our Own History"   87

CONCLUSION
The Future of the Real People   97

Notes   101
For Further Reading   104
Works Consulted   105
Index   107
Picture Credits   111
About the Author   112

Discovering the Humanity in Us All

The Way People Live series focuses on pockets of human culture. Some of these are current cultures, like the Eskimos of the Arctic; others no longer exist, such as the Jewish ghetto in Warsaw during World War II. What many of these cultural pockets share, however, is the fact that they have been viewed before, but not completely understood.

To really understand any culture, it is necessary to strip the mind of the common notions we hold about groups of people. These stereotypes are the archenemies of learning. It does not even matter whether the stereotypes are positive or negative; they are confining and tight. Removing them is a challenge that's not easily met, as anyone who has ever tried it will admit. Ideas that do not fit into the templates we create are unwelcome visitors—ones we would prefer remain quietly in a corner or forgotten room.

The cowboy of the Old West is a good example of such confining roles. The cowboy was courageous, yet soft-spoken. His time (it is always a he, in our template) was spent alternatively saving a rancher's daughter from certain death on a runaway stagecoach, or shooting it out with rustlers. At times, of course, he was likely to get a little crazy in town after a trail drive, but for the most part, he was the epitome of inner strength. It is disconcerting to find out that the cowboy is human, even a bit childish. Can it really be true that cowboys would line up to help the cook on the trail drive grind coffee, just hoping he would give them a little stick of pep-

permint candy that came with the coffee shipment? The idea of tough cowboys vying with one another to help "Coosie" (as they called their cooks) for a bit of candy seems silly and out of place.

So is the vision of Eskimos playing video games and watching MTV, living in prefab housing in the Arctic. It just does not fit with what "Eskimo" means. We are far more comfortable with snow igloos and whale blubber, harpoons and kayaks.

Although the cultures dealt with in Lucent's The Way People Live series are often historically and socially well known, the emphasis is on the personal aspects of life. Groups of people, while unquestionably affected by their politics and their governmental structures, are more than those institutions. How do people in a particular time and place educate their children? What do they eat? And how do they build their houses? What kinds of work do they do? What kinds of games do they enjoy? The answers to these questions bring these cultures to life. People's lives are revealed in the particulars and only by knowing the particulars can we understand these cultures' will to survive and their moments of weakness and greatness.

This is not to say that understanding politics does not help to understand a culture. There is no question that the Warsaw ghetto, for example, was a culture that was brought about by the politics and social ideas of Adolf Hitler and the Third Reich. But the Jews who were crowded together in the ghetto cannot be understood by the Reich's politics. Their life was a day-to-day battle for existence, and the creativity and methods they used to prolong their lives is a vital story of human perseverance that would be denied by focusing only on the institutions of Hitler's Germany. Knowing that children as young as five or six outwitted Nazi guards on a daily basis, that Jewish policemen helped the Germans control the ghetto, that children attended secret schools in the ghetto and even earned diplomas—these are the things that reveal the fabric of life, that can inspire, intrigue, and amaze.

Books in the The Way People Live series allow both the casual reader and the student to see humans as victims, heroes, and onlookers. And although humans act in ways that can fill us with feelings of sorrow and revulsion, it is important to remember that "hero," "predator," and "victim" are dangerous terms. Heaping undue pity or praise on people reduces them to objects, and strips them of their humanity.

Seeing the Jews of Warsaw only as victims is to deny their humanity. Seeing them only as they appear in surviving photos, staring at the camera with infinite sadness, is limiting, both to them and to those who want to understand them. To an object of pity, the only appropriate response becomes "Those poor creatures!" and that reduces both the quality of their struggle and the depth of their despair. No one is served by such two-dimensional views of people and their cultures.

With this in mind, the The Way People Live series strives to flesh out the traditional, two-dimensional views of people in various cultures and historical circumstances. Using a wide variety of primary quotations—the words not only of the politicians and government leaders, but of the real people whose lives are being examined—each book in the series attempts to show an honest and complete picture of a culture removed from our own by time or space.

By examining cultures in this way, the reader will notice not only the glaring differences from his or her own culture, but also will be struck by the similarities. For indeed, people share common needs—warmth, good company, stability, and affirmation from others. Ultimately, seeing how people really live, or have lived can only enrich our understanding of ourselves.

"Two Inches Above the Television Screen"

At first glance, they could be teenagers from any American city. Some carry boom boxes, others chat about a new rock video they have seen on MTV. A few have dyed their hair orange or pink; others wear their hair more conservatively. Almost all of them are wearing jeans and T-shirts with familiar designs—Nike, Hard Rock Cafe, Grateful Dead.

But a closer look would reveal that these teenagers are different. Although their homes have satellite dishes to pull in cable TV, few of them have flush toilets or running water. None of the teenagers' families owns an automobile, but all have at least one snowmobile parked outside the front door. And besides pizza and hamburgers, these teenagers frequently eat seal meat for dinner—and like it!

The World's Most Hostile Environment

These young people are Eskimos, living near or within the Arctic Circle. In the Canadian Arctic, they are known as Inupiat or Inuit; in western Alaska they are Yupik. Some

The Eskimo people inhabit the lands in and around the Arctic Circle. The map below highlights the areas of Alaska, Canada, Greenland, and Russia that are home to the world's 130,000 Eskimos.

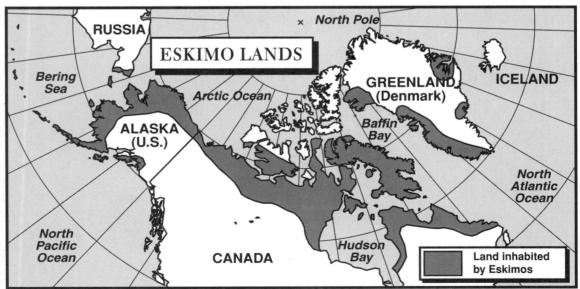

ESKIMO LANDS

RUSSIA × North Pole

Bering Sea

Arctic Ocean

ALASKA (U.S.)

GREENLAND (Denmark)

ICELAND

Baffin Bay

North Atlantic Ocean

North Pacific Ocean

CANADA

Hudson Bay

Land inhabited by Eskimos

With ingenuity and creativity, Eskimos were able to survive and adapt in the most hostile of environments. This 1926 photo of a traditional Eskimo family provides a glimpse of what life was like for the Real People for thousands of years.

Eskimos live in Greenland and Siberia. But no matter where Eskimos live, they are alike in one important respect—their homelands are scattered across the most hostile environment on earth.

In the Far North, which is home to the world's 130,000 Eskimos, it is cold most of the year. Only the months of June, July, and August have temperatures that average above freezing. The rest of the time it is bitterly cold, with temperatures sometimes reaching –70 degrees Fahrenheit. In the deepest part of winter the sun disappears entirely for months at a time. And because the territory inhabited by the Eskimos is far above the timberline—too far north for trees to grow— the frigid arctic winds blow unchecked over the ice, making the darkness and cold that much more unfriendly. It is no wonder that the first explorers to visit these northern places called them "the barrens," for it seemed that nothing could survive here.

But ever since the Eskimo people migrated across the ice from northern Asia to Alaska and Canada thousands of years ago, they have survived. In a climate with no forests or prairies filled with game, Eskimos learned to hunt whales, seals, and snow birds. In a treeless region where lumber for construction was not available, Eskimos learned how to build homes with snow and sod. And in a land that provided no easy supply of fuel, Eskimos learned how to use the oil from seals and whales to sustain the fires that heated their dwellings.

The Real People

One thing the Eskimos did not have to contend with was war. While to the south, many Native American nations were battling over land and hunting territories, no one wished to challenge the Eskimos over the ice and snow of their homelands. The two Native American nations that lived closest to the Eskimos were the Naskapi and the Cree, and neither ventured north of the timberline. It was they, in fact, who first gave these northern people the name "Eskimantsies," which means "eaters of raw meat."

The people of the Far North called themselves Inuit, Inupiat, or Yupik, which all mean, in various dialects, "the Real People." (This book uses "Eskimo," for today this term may refer to northern people who live in either Alaska or Canada.)

Through the centuries Eskimos have existed on their own, with very little influence from outside their world. Even while explorers from Europe, busy investigating the lands to the south, had begun pushing Native Americans farther and farther west, the Eskimos' world remained untouched. Strengthened by their close-knit families, the Real People needed no more than keen eyes and steady aims to hunt for food, and the wisdom of their elders to guide them.

"They Laugh at Us"

But although Eskimos were left alone longer than native people to the south, the outside world eventually crept in. And as more and more outsiders came to the Far North, they saw that the Arctic was not as barren and useless as most people had believed. The Eskimos' lands were a valuable source of great wealth—at first from whaling ships, then from fur traders, and more recently from traffickers in gold and oil.

Life in Eskimo villages has drastically changed with increased contact from outsiders, especially in the past fifty years—and some maintain that that change has been for the better. Technology never before available

Why Not?

In his book Living Arctic: Hunters of the Canadian North, *Hugh Brody examines the notions most people have about Eskimos and the Arctic lands they inhabit. It is the idea that Eskimos are somehow "lesser people," says Brody, that accounts for the reluctance of some to understand their culture.*

"Very few Europeans have been to the Arctic. It is a land without roads, has a tiny scattering of towns and the thinnest trickle of tourists. Neither has the Arctic come to us—in the way, for example, that the Orient has. We do not wear clothes made from Arctic fabrics. We do not eat Arctic foods. Very few . . . Eskimo words have entered the English language. Furs, whale oil, and whalebone have, of course, played their part in European history. The men who brought these goods to Europe have been celebrated as great adventurers and heroes. But even the voracious . . . appetites of European culture have found little or nothing in Arctic cultures to absorb and make their own.

Nevertheless, the far north has been a focus of intense interest for at least four centuries. As imagery and metaphor, as challenge and menace, as romance and adventure, the Arctic worked as keenly on the European imagination as any other geographical region. How are we to explain this combination of distance and proximity, cultural separation and obsession?"

to the Eskimo people is now commonplace in northern villages. Powerful motorboats have largely replaced the traditional kayaks and umiaks, the precisely engineered, skin-covered boats used for hunting. It's much more common to see a sleek, modern snowmobile than a team of sled dogs outside the home of an Eskimo hunter. Modern medicine can cure Eskimo children of diseases that only a few generations ago would have killed them. Once a culture that was on the move, following the migratory patterns of the animals on which they depended, the Eskimos now live in permanent villages. Famine and mass starvation are a thing of the past.

But many feel that Eskimos in Alaska and the Canadian Arctic lost more than they gained by their new relationship with the outside world. Few hunt to feed their families; instead, people rely on canned and frozen food from village grocery stores. As a result, many of the skills that used to be handed down from generation to generation are being lost. Alcoholism is epidemic; the use of drugs like cocaine and crack is growing among the young people. And the stories and songs of the elders are taking a backseat to video games.

Many Eskimos worry about the future of their culture. Exposure via television to the material culture of the United States and Canada has made many young Eskimos embarrassed and ashamed of their lifestyle. "The world thinks we live in snow igloos and

While the Eskimo way of life remained virtually undisturbed for centuries, it has undergone drastic change in the past fifty years. This modern Eskimo village reflects many of the changes that have taken place. It bears little resemblance to the igloo villages of the past.

"They Have to Make Choices"

In a World Press Review *article called "Between Hunting and Hard Rock," Carole Beaulieu describes a modern Inuit community in Canada. As this quotation shows, today's Canadian Eskimos have very difficult choices to make in a world that is both modern and traditional.*

"The old folks in the Canadian Arctic once lived in igloos and remember the big hunts, epidemics, and famines. They saw the white people arrive and build houses, schools, and hospitals, bringing with them electricity, television, pizzerias, and heated sports arenas.

Today, the Inuit population is growing four times faster than the national average—a real 'baby boom,' brought about by declining infant mortality. Caught between seal-hunting and pop music, between harpoons and computers, young Inuit feel that they are living in two worlds. 'Their fathers were hunters,' says George Qulaut, an Inuk coordinator at the Igloolik research center. 'But they cannot be hunters. Not full time. They have to make choices their parents did not have to make.' In the North, schoolrooms are plastered with posters against drugs, tobacco, and alcohol. An official in the town of Cambridge Bay says that even crack has made its way to the pole."

chew cold whale meat or something," says an Inuit teen. "They laugh at us. Those kids [in Canada and the United States] don't think we're like them at all, but we are."[1]

Many young Inuit agree. It's hard, they say, for those who live outside their world to understand them. And how could they, wonders one Inuit girl, when the Eskimo world is so remote that it is almost invisible to outsiders? The world map used to show weather patterns and world events doesn't even show the Arctic homeland of the Real People. "I live in those two inches above the television screen," this perceptive teenager laughs. "I live in the two inches of Canada that you can't see."[2]

Between Two Skins

In the Inuit language, the word *aqunnaaki*, which means, literally, "between two skins," is used to refer to teenagers. They are neither grownups nor children—they are in two separate worlds, not at home in either one. Those who have taken time to learn about the Eskimos say that in many ways, *all* Eskimos are *aqunnaaki*—they are between the "skins" of the old, familiar culture of their elders and the new, modern way of life.

What is life like in an Eskimo village today? What are the ancient traditions that are still followed? How do people keep those traditions alive, when the modern world seems so appealing? Is it possible for a balance to be struck between the old and the new? Or is there no room today for the Real People?

Traditions of the Real People

It is impossible to understand the troubles in Eskimo villages today without recognizing the conflict between the old and new. The old customs and traditions—many of which are still followed—have been the backbone of Eskimo culture for thousands of years, and the changes have been amazingly slight. "They knew no outsiders, no one different from themselves," writes Aylette Jenness, who has studied the Yupik Eskimos. "During those hundreds and hundreds of years, their way of life changed very little. People followed in the footsteps of their ancestors, children learning from their parents the vast body of knowledge necessary for survival in this environment."[3]

What are these time-tested traditions, which seem to be on a collision course with modern ideas? And how could they have stayed so constant over the centuries?

Survival

It seems almost too simple, but the most important reason for Eskimo customs and traditions can be summed up in one word: survival. Whereas in some societies, traditions are maintained because of religious beliefs or national pride, or because they are imposed by those in power, Eskimo traditions are necessary for the survival of the group. Without them, the Real People would cease to exist.

Eskimo hunters, pulled by sled dogs, weather the harsh cold in search of food. In an environment that provided little for its inhabitants, survival was a way of life for the Eskimos.

Because of the extreme cold in and around the Arctic Circle, the entire activity of the traditional Eskimo people revolved around two main tasks: staying warm and finding food. They had what is known as a "subsistence" way of life—everything they needed came from the land. Food, clothing, housing materials, things used to create their art—all came from the land and sea of the Far North.

But the Far North was stingy with what it provided. There were limits to the number of animals a hunter could find there, and to the kinds of material suitable for building a warm home. And because resources for making warm homes and clothing were limited, and hunting in frigid temperatures was extremely difficult, the Eskimos had to rely on innovation and creativity.

The Northern Diet

Throughout the history of the Eskimos, widespread starvation has been a fact of life. Poor hunting conditions, or a scarcity of game—whatever the reasons, the Eskimos had no alternative to their subsistence life. If the seal or the whale could not be killed, families had nothing to eat. There were no stores, no people nearby who could help in emergencies. The Eskimos were quite alone. Even today, when few Eskimos follow a subsistence lifestyle, elders in their communities tell of whole villages being wiped out because people were unable to find sufficient food.

James Houston, a writer who lived for many years among the Eskimos, recalled being stunned by the extreme hunger of the people in one village in 1950. "I'll tell you what hungry is," Houston recalls. "When we arrived, we had some tea leaves that had been rewatered in a bucket for five or six days, getting paler and paler. I scooped out

the leaves and threw them on the snow. The camp kids rushed out and ate them."[4]

The Yupiks and other Eskimos below the Arctic Circle had a few more choices than the Eskimos farther north. Besides whale and seal, they hunted birds, fished in rivers and along the seacoast, and collected clams, berries, and edible plants. But the northernmost Eskimo people ate mainly walrus, seal, and the fish swimming below the ice. A few land mammals were hunted, such as polar bear and caribou (large deer), but these were of interest more for their furs and hides than for their meat.

Most of the game animals were on the move. They migrated for warmth during intense cold, and sometimes to evade the presence of the Eskimo hunters. Their migration forced the Eskimos to migrate, too. The history of the Eskimo people has been one of movement, of following the animals on which they depend.

"Where Are You Staying?"

Because of this nomadic existence, the idea of "home" for Eskimos has rarely been represented by a fixed place. There was territory, and within a large expanse of it, the Eskimos felt at home. Home was not a particular house.

"Home is the territory as a whole," writes one who has studied Eskimo people. "Many [Eskimos] when speaking English will ask, 'Where are you staying?' in contexts when Europeans and North Americans would ask 'Where do you live?'"[5]

It is little wonder, then, that Eskimos traditionally had many homes—a new dwelling each time they moved. Often the dwellings were used from year to year, as a family returned to a familiar hunting territory. However this was not always the case; an

Until recently the Eskimos were a nomadic people; migration was necessary for survival. Here, an Eskimo family migrates inland with their few belongings in tow.

empty dwelling was understood to be available for anyone to use, since no ownership was attached to a given structure once the family occupying it had moved on.

During the long winter, most Eskimos built their homes on the thick ice of the sea, to be as close as possible to their food source. Even Eskimos who lived most of the year inland migrated toward the water as winter approached. The animals that could provide food and fur for their existence during warmer months would be scarce throughout the wickedly cold winters. But while food might be more plentiful near the sea, the blasting wind was more violent, blowing unchecked along miles of flat arctic ice. What houses did the Eskimos build that could keep them alive in such conditions?

The Sod Igloo

It is a common—but incorrect—notion that in winter Eskimos build their houses of blocks of snow, those round snow domes we

know as "igloos." Actually, the word *igloo* in the language of many Eskimos refers to any dwelling, not just a house made of snow. Only a very small percentage of Eskimos lived in snow igloos—most preferred a different kind of winter home.

Most of the winter dwellings were constructed with frames of whalebone or stone, or large pieces of wood that had drifted to shore from wrecked ships. The outside of the house was covered with turf or sod, and packed on top with blankets of snow. The walls were double-thick, stones or wood, with a warm insulating layer of sod between.

"We lived in a sod house," remembers Mary Ann Sundown, a Yupik grandmother from Alaska. "The insides of our house had braided grass hanging on the walls as paneling. We had only one window, which was made out of dried seal guts, and it made a lot of noise when it was windy."[6]

The sod house had one main room, with one or two smaller rooms on each side for storage, or for butchering animals. The entrance was roundabout—a long tunnel led

The Snow Igloo

Although the snow igloo has become a stereotypical home for all Eskimos, only those in the Central Arctic used snow houses as their ordinary winter dwelling. Still, the knowledge of how to construct one was important, for the ability to erect a warm home with the materials at hand could save a hunter's life in any part of the Arctic. In his book The Eskimos, *Ernest S. Burch Jr. describes this most interesting of Eskimo houses.*

"The material required to make a snow house is hard, wind-packed snow. Snow is comprised of tiny air pockets, which make it an excellent insulating material. If it has been packed into drifts under the proper wind conditions, it is also easy to extract and shape with the aid of a special knife. . . .

A dome snow house was an architectural masterpiece, and it required considerable skill to construct. The builder had to know how to assess the properties of drifted snow, he had to be able to estimate the size of the ring for the foundation layer, he had to gauge the inward slope of the blocks so that

Hard snow is the only material necessary for building a snow igloo. However, the considerable skill required takes years of practice.

they would converge at precisely the right place at the top without collapsing during the construction process, and he had to cut out and shape each individual block without a template or other guide. Such skill took years of observation and practice to acquire."

in from outside. This arrangement eliminated the need for a front door, through which precious heat from inside the house would have been lost each time someone went in or out. The tunnel was not only long, it was low—so low that one entering the house had to crawl. Just before the tunnel met the main room, there was an entryway with a much higher ceiling. Here each member of the family would brush snow crystals off clothing before coming into the house. Otherwise, the dry

snow of the Arctic would soon melt, soaking clothing and skin—a dangerous condition when temperatures plummeted to –70 degrees and windchill reached a deadly –150 degrees! Although the houses were warm, it would have been suicidal to dress in still-wet clothing the next time it was necessary to leave the house.

Inside the sod igloo a fire and cooking area took up the middle of the main room. The ground was covered with stones or

Contrary to popular belief, most Eskimos lived not in snow igloos but in sod houses like the one seen here. The sod served as a layer of insulation to keep the house warm.

pieces of wood. Comfort was not important, for this floor area was used only for walking and sometimes for butchering animals for the food supply. All other activities took place on platforms, raised several inches above the floor. The platforms were made of stone or wood, like the floor, but were covered with layers of sod and piles of warm furs. This is where the family slept, ate their meals, and spent their time when they weren't outdoors.

Lamps

Eskimos traditionally depended on lamps for indoor heating and lighting. Most lamps were made of clay or carved soapstone, a soft rock.

Eskimo culture assigned different tasks to men and women, and the lighting and tending of the lamp was no exception. The woman's job was to prepare the lamp, so that her husband could light it. Once lit, the lamp was again the woman's responsibility. That responsibility was no small thing—a lamp that burned too slowly resulted in a cold, uncomfortable house.

To prepare the lamp, an Eskimo woman would take a piece of seal fat—called blubber—and chew it slightly, so that the oil inside oozed to the surface. Then she set into the lamp, upright next to the fat, a wick made of rolled and twisted moss. Next her husband would light the lamp. Since Eskimos had no matches until trade began with outsiders, this step required special effort.

Seal oil lamps, like the one used here, provided vital heat and light in the otherwise cold, dark igloos.

An Inuit demonstrates how a bow drill is used to drill a hole. Similar tools were used to start fires before the acquisition of matches from outside traders.

Most of the time, Eskimos relied on a tool called a bow drill to start fires. This was a pointed stick, which the user held vertically between his knees. The sharp point of the stick rested lightly on a piece of soft wood, and this was close to some kindling—usually a handful of dry grass, or sometimes the filmy tassels of the Arctic cotton plant, which is abundant in much of the Canadian North. By spinning the stick very quickly against the soft wood, the Eskimo produced friction, in turn generating enough heat to strike a spark that would set the kindling on fire. The newly kindled fire was then used to light the lamp.

Very few Eskimos today use soapstone seal oil lamps, but those who have memories of them say that the lamps gave off a tremendous amount of heat. So warm was the house—even in the coldest winter weather—that Eskimos stripped down to a single layer of clothing inside, and were more than comfortable.

But as efficient as the seal oil lamp was in old Eskimo homes, the fuel was not clean. Archaeologists recently discovered a prehistoric Eskimo house near Barrow, Alaska, in which several well-preserved bodies lay. Autopsies revealed that all these ancient people had suffered from breathing problems similar to "black lung disease," which plagues coal miners. The lungs were full of black soot from a lifetime of inhaling the burning seal oil.

More Troublesome than the Cold

The sod igloos were abandoned as soon as spring came to the Far North, for Eskimo families moved inland in search of other kinds of game during warm weather. Summer homes were tents, made of the skin of seal or caribou. Hair was carefully scraped from the hides to make the tents lighter and easier to transport from place to place.

Summer tents were held up by poles made of whalebone or, if a family was lucky enough to have found suitable pieces of driftwood, wood. The sides were not pegged down, as many tents are, for pegs would not hold in the hard, rocky ground of the Arctic and subarctic. Instead, heavy rocks ringed the tent bottom, acting as weights to keep it from blowing away.

The interior of an Eskimo summer tent was similar to that of a sod house, except that the eating and sleeping area was not raised on a platform. The seal oil lamp was used in the summer, too, for nights were often chilly. The tent was pleasant, except for the constant presence of mosquitoes, which the Eskimos hated. One scholar specializing in Eskimo traditions found that Eskimos universally despised the hordes of mosquitoes that plagued them throughout the summer months. While one might suppose that the frigid temperatures of the North would be the most hated feature of the Eskimos' environment, says Ernest S. Burch Jr., "temperature ranked a distant fourth to mosquitoes, rain, and wind as an annoyance."[7]

The insects were not only relentless, they were dangerous. They swarmed around mouths and noses, often suffocating small children who could not wave them away fast enough. But even the adults weren't quick enough to completely escape attack—many spent the summer months with faces swollen by bloody welts. Nothing could keep all the mosquitoes away, but most Eskimos lit fires of scrub willow outside, near the entrance to their tents. The fire forced the people inside to lie on the floor to avoid breathing the heavy, acrid smoke, but many mosquitoes stayed away. The Eskimos also fashioned thin mosquito netting from the hair of musk oxen. Most tents had at least one mosquito swatter made of the light, strong skin of birds.

Humans were not the only ones bothered by the mosquitoes. One Eskimo elder from northern Canada recalls how the insects tormented his dogs, and how he dealt with that problem. "Lots of mosquitoes when we walk," he writes. "Arraa! There were so many mosquitoes, I had a five-gallon can of seal oil that I took so I could rub my dogs' noses and faces and legs and thin spots. . . . When you don't rub them, they begin to holler a little bit when mosquitoes poke their needles right inside. . . . Their noses start to swell up."[8]

A young Inuit gazes out from his family's tent. Used as summer dwellings, these light, easily transportable tents were made from the skin of seal or caribou.

One Occupation Only

But as important as it was to build and maintain a warm, snug home in the Far North, food was always a more pressing need. For a traditional Eskimo man, hunting was the only occupation available. If he was a poor hunter, or a lazy one, he died—and his family died with him. There was simply no other choice.

Interestingly, hunting was *not* an option for Eskimo women. It was considered bad luck for a woman even to touch a bow and arrow or a harpoon. As the author of a very well researched novel on Eskimo life states, "If a woman tried to harpoon an animal herself, the hunters believed that other animals would stay away and that everyone would starve."[9] The harsh, difficult life of the Arctic seemed to demand that the roles of women and men remain very well defined. The women cooked, sewed, and cleaned the game their husbands killed. The men's primary role was hunter.

Important to Eskimos, seals were hunted year round and were used for meat, clothing, and tools.

For food, most Eskimos depended on sea mammals—seals, whales, walruses. Of those, the quarry most sought by Eskimos, no matter what the season, was seal. Some anthropologists who have studied traditional Eskimos say that seals were to them as the buffalo were to many Native American tribes of the plains. Seal meat made up the bulk of their diet, and other parts of the animal were used for clothing, tools, rope, and home furnishings.

Seals were hunted all year round—in the winter from the ice, and in warmer months, from boats, the kayaks or umiaks. But in any season, seal hunting could be agonizingly difficult, a perfect illustration of the magnitude of the task of survival.

Hunting the Breathing Holes

In winter, seal hunting was a waiting game lasting hours, or even days, in the endless arctic darkness. Seals live underwater, surfacing only briefly every seven or eight minutes for a gulp of air before diving again. The ice is often four or five feet thick—like a hard white marble floor. The bell-shaped breathing holes are seal-made, scooped out by the sharp claws of the seals' flippers. Each seal may have two dozen breathing holes, which it visits regularly—either to grab a breath or for maintenance purposes (that is, to keep the holes free of ice buildup).

The breathing holes on the ice, although numerous, are small and difficult to see; it takes a practiced eye to notice them. Often Eskimos relied on their dogs' sense of smell to locate the holes. But finding a breathing hole was just the beginning. It was necessary for the hunter to stay perfectly still by the edge of the little opening, waiting for the seal to surface.

A hunter, harpoon in hand, waits quietly by a breathing hole for a seal to surface. This hunting method requires a great deal of skill and patience.

Noise was the enemy—any sort of noise. Seals have incredibly sharp ears: even under several feet of ice they can distinguish footsteps high above. For this reason, hunters wore soft soles of bear fur or caribou skin to muffle their movements. They even laced down their clothes with leather thongs to keep them from flapping in the sharp wind.

The difficult part was the waiting. The hunter knew that a seal would come to the hole, but he had no way of predicting when. He had no choice but to sit by the breathing hole, harpoon in hand, and try to stay warm and alert. Sam Hall, who has studied the Eskimos, describes the hunter as

> a shapeless huddle of white, his clothing encrusted with a thin film of rime frost and his face, eyebrows, mustache, and beard glittering in the moonlight with the frozen moisture of his breath. . . . His eyes, mere slits in the freezing cold. In the darkness and the mind-numbing cold, it was easy to fall into a semi-comatose state, so he would force himself to concentrate and stay awake.[10]

To give himself a small advantage in predicting the seal's arrival, the hunter inserted a long stalk of grass or a thin sliver of bone into the hole. When the float bobbed suddenly, it was certain that the seal was about to surface, and the hunter would explode into action, hoping that his aim was true. If he missed, or if the harpoon did not strike the neck or skull of the seal, the animal would struggle to escape. And since most adult seals weigh about one hundred pounds, the man was in danger of being pulled down through the breathing hole and into the icy water—a certain death.

On the other hand, writes Hall, "a spreading stain of red told him that his aim had been precise, that the barbed harpoon had struck the seal in the nape of the neck, and killed it with a single blow."[11] After enlarging the breathing hole with a knife, the hunter would hoist the seal up onto the ice and drag it home.

Nothing Wasted

The hunter's immediate reward (other than satisfaction for a job well done) was a quick meal of seal's liver. The liver was eaten raw—either alone, or mixed with a few small pieces of fat—while the seal's body was still warm. Then the rest of the animal was skinned and butchered by the hunter's wife. She used an *ulu,* a razor-sharp knife shaped like a crescent. Some of the meat was eaten that night, but most was dried in long strips, smoked, and stored for another day.

And it was not only the meat that was taken. Every part of the animal, except for

A woman cuts sealskin to make boots with a crescent-shaped ulu *knife. The* ulu *was a valuable tool used to skin and butcher animals.*

lungs, genitals, and a few little scraps of intestine, was used for something. Nothing was wasted—that was the Eskimo way. One writer found that same rule applied to fish, birds, and any other animal killed by Eskimo hunters, and the uses were often highly inventive.

> Brains are rubbed into hides as a skin softener and preservative. Spinal and leg tendons are used to make thread. Seal windpipes and intestines can serve as [igloo] windows. Fish skins can be turned into strong and compact needle and fishhook cases. [Bird] bladders make children's balloons. Fish eyes are a treat—rather like snacks for children. Boiled ducks' feet are fun to eat. The bones of a seal's flipper made all the pieces for an elaborate [Eskimo] game.[12]

Grass in Their Boots and Feathered Underwear

Of all the uses for animals besides food, however, clothing ranked at the very top. Since so much Eskimo activity took place outdoors, clothing had to keep the people warm and dry. It is difficult to imagine how any clothing—except maybe some high-tech, space-age garments—could keep people comfortable in the frigid temperatures of the Arctic. But Eskimos were observant, creative people, and through many centuries of living in the most difficult climate on earth, they had learned how to make clothing that was more suitable than anything the modern world could offer.

The first European explorers to the Arctic described the Eskimos they encountered as fat. In fact, however, as a group, these northern people are thin and wiry. It was their loose-fitting clothing that gave the Eskimos a roly-poly appearance. If used

Arriving in the Arctic

Between the years 1877 and 1881, Edward William Nelson lived among the Bering Sea Eskimos in what is now Alaska. In Inua: Spirit World of the Bering Sea Eskimo, *editors William W. Fitzhugh and Susan A. Kaplan include Nelson's description of the Arctic landscape as he first arrived.*

"At length a breeze arose, and during the pale twilight of the next midnight we forced a passage through a scattered ice-pack. During all of my experiences in this region I never saw equaled the gorgeous coloring exhibited on this night by sea or sky. Along the northern horizon, where the sun crept just out of sight, lay a bank of broken clouds tinged fiery red and edged with golden and purple shades.

Floating about us in stately array were the fantastic forms of the sea ice, exhibiting the most intense shades of green and blue, and the sea, for a time nearly black, slowly became a sullen green, on which the white caps chased one another in quick succession.

As the sun neared the horizon the rosy flush spread from the clouds to the sky all around and a purple tint touched the sea and ice in to the most gorgeous coloring, which lasted for an hour. The rush of the waves among the fragments of ice and the grinding of the pieces among themselves and along the side of the vessel made a strange monotone that blended harmoniously with the mysterious brooding twilight and the rare coloring of sea and sky."

properly, layers of clothing weighing less than ten pounds could keep an Eskimo hunter warm enough to sleep outdoors in –60 degree Fahrenheit weather with no other protection.

The Eskimos found that feathers of certain species of birds—especially ducks and geese—were excellent insulators. So, for the first layer of clothing, they wore undershirts made of bird skin, worn in reverse, with the feathers next to the skin. Quite possibly the fanciest undershirt ever devised, each bird feather garment was made up of the skins and feathers of one hundred different birds.

The undershirt fit loosely, for it was very important that clothing not trap perspiration next to the skin. If moisture accumulated on the skin, the clothing would become soaked and would soon freeze. Hypothermia (loss of body heat) would follow, and then certain death. To prevent this from happening, Eskimos wore all their clothing loose, allowing air to circulate underneath, while still retaining body warmth. The fear of what perspiration could do was so prevalent, in fact, that Eskimos took other precautions to keep themselves from getting too warm. To keep from getting overheated, Eskimo hunters always moved at a slow, smooth pace, rather than a fast walk.

The outer two layers of clothing were skins of fox, ground squirrel, mink, caribou, or even polar bear. The outer layer was worn with the fur on the outside, the inner layer with the fur closest to the skin. The garments were sewn with thread made of seal and caribou tendon, using bone needles.

Making clothing of skins is difficult because uncured leather is board-stiff. A woman could not use her needle to sew until the skins were softened—and that task was done not by hand, but by mouth. For hours, and often days, Eskimo women chewed animal skins until they were soft and supple, and could be sewn easily.

So effective was this chewing, in fact, that many Eskimo men asked their wives to soften all of the clothing the same way. In the evenings, while the men repaired tools or played with the children, Eskimo women chewed the family's leather garments to

Eskimo women spent many hours chewing tough leather hides to make them soft and supple. Softer hides were easier to sew and more comfortable to wear.

Frigid temperatures in the Arctic require warm clothing. Loose-fitting clothing like that worn by this man gave the Eskimos their deceptively roly-poly appearance.

make them more comfortable for the next day's wear. Skeletal remains of Eskimo women from many centuries ago show the teeth of old women all but worn down to nubs—proof of the amount of leather chewing done in a lifetime.

Eskimos wore long boots made of sealskin, waterproofed by soaking in urine and seal oil. Since toes were highly vulnerable to frostbite, it was very important to keep feet warm. Thus each morning a layer of dried grass was placed in the sole, to provide an extra layer of insulation. (During the warmer summer months, grass was cut and saved for just this purpose.)

The Mark of Success

Because the Eskimos were a nomadic people, a reliable means of transportation was essential. The dogsled served this need; historians maintain that the Inuit and other Canadian Arctic Eskimos would have died out, had it not been for their dogs. The teams of dogs used both to pull sleds and to help sniff out game were a key part of traditional Eskimo culture.

An Eskimo kept as many dogs as he could afford to feed. For that reason, dogs were a status symbol in most Eskimo communities. A team of one or two thin, scraggly animals was a sign of a poor hunter. On the other hand, an Eskimo who could keep eight or ten dogs sleek and well-fed was obviously a skilled and brave provider. As one expert on traditional Eskimos writes, "Each hunter took pride in displaying his team to neighbors and travelers, who offered advice and

"A Weird, Wild Harmony"

Nineteenth-century anthropologist Edward William Nelson found that the Eskimos' dogs played a very important role in the life of the community. Not only did they work hard, they even provided their owners with a strange chorus of music, as Nelson relates in Inua: Spirit World of the Bering Sea Eskimo, *edited by William W. Fitzhugh and Susan A. Kaplan.*

"In winter, the hunter is accompanied by his sledge [sled] and dogs on every important hunt. The dogs are invaluable aids in finding game in many cases, and are used to drag it homeward across the icy hummocks or snowy plains. They haul the sledges laden with household goods and children when a change of abode becomes necessary, and are ever at hand for the unstinted amount of work heaped upon them, spiced with a plenitude of kicks and blows. . . .

The moon has great influence over the dogs, and during full moon half the night is passed by them howling in chorus. During the entire winter at Saint Michaels we were invariably given a chorus every moonlight night, and the dogs of two neighboring villages joined in the serenade. Their howl is a long-drawn cry, rising and falling in somewhat regular cadence. The chorus of a hundred dogs, slightly softened by the distance, has a weird, wild harmony in keeping with the surroundings, and produces a strong and stirring effect upon the listener."

Invaluable during hunts, sled dogs were also known to provide a howling chorus of music during a full moon.

discussed each dog, as a typical huddle of racing enthusiasts might weigh the merits of a thoroughbred."[13]

The dogs were not pets, they were working animals. Even so, they were treated with respect. Eskimo hunters were aware of how important the dogs were to their survival. They were fed before the family, and they ate the same foods—fish, seal, walrus. Historians agree that Eskimos honored no one more than their dogs—except their sons.

Eskimo sled dogs were bred from Siberian huskies and wolves. They possessed the best characteristics of both animals—speed, endurance, and strength. The dogs were usually gray; however they were sometimes white with red or yellow fur. Each full-grown dog could pull eighty pounds—a team of ten dogs could travel forty miles in a day pulling eight hundred pounds.

A valued part of traditional Eskimo culture, sled dogs were a status symbol in most Eskimo communities. The more dogs a man had, the greater a hunter he was assumed to be.

Appreciation, Not Soft-Heartedness

Even though the Eskimos honored their dogs, they were in no way soft-hearted in their treatment of these animals. Survival was not guaranteed to anyone in the Arctic—and the sled dogs were no exception.

Just after birth, puppies were examined by the Eskimo hunter, and only those that seemed strong were allowed to live. "Robust puppies, when held up by the scruff of their necks for inspection," writes one Eskimo expert, "arched their backs and struggled furiously. Weak puppies hung limply. These were thrown back to the mother and the pack and were devoured in seconds."[14]

The puppies that survived had to undergo some dentistry at the hands of their Eskimo masters as soon as their permanent teeth came in. To prevent them from chewing through their leather harnesses and leads, the hunter filed each puppy's teeth down with a rock. Having dull-toothed dogs meant more work for him, however, for he had to cut up all the dogs' food into bite-sized chunks. Otherwise, without their sharp chewing teeth, the dogs would have had to swallow their food whole.

The dogs worked hardest away from the igloo, on a winter hunting expedition. The dogs always slept outdoors, but when traveling, they did not even have the protection of the windbreak of the Eskimo's home. Ears down, they tucked their noses under their tails and waited out the fiercest storms—often for days at a time. Feeding was not a daily occurrence, either. Eskimos found that their dogs performed better when hungry, and so a meal every two or three days was deemed sufficient.

One bonus of being away from home that the dogs truly enjoyed—although we might

During hunting expeditions sled dogs often went for days without food, and were forced to sleep outdoors with no protection from even the fiercest of storms.

shudder to imagine it—was the daily supply of human excrement. Eskimo sled dogs seemed to have a real taste for it, and fought among themselves each time the hunter relieved himself—much to the man's dismay. As one writer jokes, "The cold does not encourage a . . . driver to waste time while performing the requirements of nature. A pack of dogs fighting voraciously at his heels in order to wolf down a warm meal made speed imperative."[15]

Although the solitary time a hunter spent out on the winter ice was peaceful, Eskimos have always been very social people. The most enjoyable parts of their lives were those spent with family and friends. Community was vital, not only to their emotional well-being, but to their physical survival—as much as food, shelter, warm clothing, and the service of a loyal team of sled dogs.

CHAPTER 2

For the Good of the Community

Traditional Eskimo families were very self-sufficient. A husband and wife, working together, could build their home, hunt for food, make clothing, and raise a family, but such an existence would have been very tenuous. If the husband died, his isolated survivors would soon perish for lack of food. If the woman were to die, the man would have no one to butcher the meat, make clothing, and keep the house warm.

The Eskimo Community

Because of the risk associated with living in a single-family group in the Arctic, Eskimos have traditionally lived in bands, or small groups. Each band was made up of several extended families, including grandparents, cousins, aunts, and uncles. Usually twenty to forty people lived in a band, most of them related at least by marriage. Orphans or widows would not need to fear starvation in such a community.

The band of Eskimos was also part of a larger group, who in their hunting and migrating moved in the same general area. A band of Eskimos was likely to meet up with others in their group once or twice during the year, and the relationships were usually very friendly.

Groups might be as small as a hundred people, or as large as a thousand. Eskimo groups were not formal associations—no laws or treaties bound them together. In many cases, members of various bands were related. But there were even stronger ties—the customs and traditions the people shared.

Eskimos traditionally lived in bands, which were made up of several extended families. Band members shared strong ties, and decisions were always made for the good of the whole community.

Pretending to Hunt

In the book Canada North of Sixty, *edited by Jergen Boden and Elke Boden, an Inuit woman named Ann Meekitjuk Hanson remembers that although the times when families relied solely on the hunters for food were difficult, they were not without their lighter moments.*

"When I think back, I remember the young men walked to hunt for small game. That was part of their education. Small game included ptarmigans [birds like grouses], fish, foxes. My brother Egeesiaq used to walk. Sometimes he would come back empty-handed. When he came back with ptarmigans, they were shared by everyone in the camp. Years later, my brother candidly confessed that he sometimes pretended he was hunting. He would walk just outside the camp, sit down, observe the camp, have a rest. When he thought he had been gone long enough, he walked back to camp. Then he would relate his hunting 'expedition' sorrowfully, saying, 'The ptarmigans were too timid today' or 'There was too much wind.' Today he says, 'I was just being lazy!' in which case we bellow out with laughter."

Eskimos were very different from other native people, in that they had no chiefs, or leaders, in their bands. There was no government, no council, no voting on what the group should do, or where they should hunt. No one was elected to tell others what they must or must not do.

There were unofficial leaders, however. The bravest and most successful hunter in the band was entitled to respect, and was often consulted on matters that related to the group as a whole. But in no way would he expect others to follow his suggestions—compliance was totally voluntary. As one Eskimo says, "When an Inuk [Eskimo] wants to hunt, he hunts; he does not need to be told by other people."[16]

So foreign was the idea of an authority or "man in charge" in Eskimo communities that there was no word for it in Inuit or Yupik languages. The closest term, in one Canadian Eskimo dialect, means "a very bossy one," and was used as an insult.

Thinking of the Community

The notion that one person could be more important than his or her peers has always been distasteful to Eskimos, for it goes against what they held as most important—community. Survival could occur only within the group, with everyone doing his or her part. Pride, arrogance, self-importance—these were all poisonous, for they replaced a sense of care and concern for the community.

For that reason, in traditional Eskimo communities individualism was not a positive trait. Even language reflects this notion. It was rare to hear the first-person pronoun "I" in a sentence, for that would indicate that an Eskimo was thinking in terms of himself or herself. "An [Eskimo] would seldom say, 'I am leaving,' but 'Somebody here is going for a walk,'" writes one Eskimo historian. "The wife of a destitute hunter confronted with an empty larder would not ask 'What can I do?' but 'How can a poor woman cook when there is no food in the house?'" [17]

Another sure sign that individualism was discouraged in Eskimo societies is the absence of ownership. Individuals owned very little—a few tools, perhaps, but those could be replaced. There was no currency, no money to save and spend. Houses were used, not owned—when a family left a home (which they might or might not have built) it was understood that anyone who needed it could move in.

Even land was not owned, at least not in the sense that we speak of ownership today. A hunter talked about land being his if he had a relationship with the land, if he or his ancestors had hunted and fished there. There were no deeds or titles, no boundaries separating one Eskimo group's territory from another's.

"I Always Give It, If I Have It"

But there was no more obvious sign of an Eskimo's respect of the community than in the way food was distributed. James Houston, who lived for many years in Eskimo communities, was impressed with their unselfishness when it came to food—surprising in a culture in which starvation was a constant danger. "They taught me about kindness," he says, "about generosity from one human being to another—a generosity of a kind I couldn't believe. An Eskimo would share his last goose egg with you when food was scarce." [18]

Whenever an Eskimo hunter killed an animal, the first thing he did was share with others. Anyone who needed food got a share of the meat—women without husbands, other hunters who had not been successful that day. Before the hunter and his family enjoyed a meal, the choicest portions were given away. To be able to share was considered an honor, rather than a duty. The hunter who shared was obviously skilled, and was worthy of the respect of his community.

A hunter skins a wolf while his wife and daughter look on. After killing an animal, a hunter always gave away the choicest portions before feeding his own family.

No one had to ask a hunter to share. It was simply understood that that was how people behaved. As one hunter who still lives by that rule explains:

When anyone comes asking for something, I always give it, if I have it. It doesn't matter if they can't repay you. Ever since I can remember, my mother always used to tell me that, even if I did not have very much, as long as I had a bit to share, and saw someone without anything to eat, she would like me to share with them. That was how I was brought up.[19]

In Inuit communities, meat that had been distributed to various families was placed on a rack outside the igloo, high enough to escape the hungry dogs. It was not considered stealing, however, for an Eskimo to climb on another family's rack and take down meat that had been allotted to that family. If someone needed it badly enough, it was right that he or she should have it.

Dealing with Trouble

Some Eskimos did not honor these unselfish traditions, however. Sometimes people were selfish, or arrogant. Sometimes people were lazy, or took more than their share. Problems arising from such behavior needed to be confronted and resolved. How could the Eskimo community, which had neither written laws nor civic leaders, deal with personal conflicts?

In Eskimo tradition, it was considered rude to directly confront another person, or to get visibly angry. Eskimos preferred to ignore an unpleasant situation, hoping that the offending party, seeing the foolishness of his or her ways, would voluntarily reform. As

James Houston noted, "If an Eskimo meets someone who doesn't seem worthwhile, he says, 'What a waste of time!' If an Eskimo is angry, he doesn't stay to fight, he slides out of your life. They try to keep gossip kindly, they make only subtle digs, because they have to rely on each other."[20]

How to keep the mood light, but still resolve the problem? One of the most effective weapons in resolving problems was teasing. Like most people, Eskimos hated being laughed at or teased. If someone was acting selfishly, or in a way that did not benefit the community, his family and friends were quick to poke fun at him. Usually this was not done cruelly, for it was important that the person be able to save face by laughing along with the joke. For instance, if someone had taken more meat than he needed, as one historian points out, "he would soon be ridiculed, and taunted as a worthless, improvident hunter. 'Is the hunting so poor that an [Eskimo] cannot provide himself with so much as a seabird?' his neighbors would cry."[21]

Often two Eskimos having a dispute would settle it by means of a contest in which they took turns singing insults to each other. The community would watch and laugh as the contestants made fun of each other's looks, hunting ability, mothers' cooking, or anything else they could think of. The winner was decided by the onlookers, who would cheer and applaud the one who sang the funniest and most creative insult songs.

Occasionally, ridicule did not work, and offenders would continue in their selfish ways. In such cases, the entire community simply turned their backs on them, as though they did not exist. No one replied when they asked a question or made a comment. They were not included in activities. Historians say that being ignored was such a painful

A game of teasing was often used to settle disputes among Eskimos. Community members watched as each party took turns insulting one another. The winner, selected by the onlookers, was the one with the most humorous and creative insults.

experience that many ostracized Eskimos ended up setting off on their own, and usually died without the support of the group.

Rarely Violent

In rare instances—a murder or rape, perhaps—an offender was killed. The Eskimos did not look at such a violent punishment with horror or even regret. It was simply an act that needed to be done, justified because the community had been threatened. Nothing, and no one, was more important than the community.

Sometimes such action was taken against people who were not members of the Eskimo community. For example, in 1913 two Canadian Eskimos killed two priests who had attempted to force them at gunpoint to make a journey the Eskimos believed was too dangerous. Twelve years later, an Inuit hunter killed a white fur trader. The trader had been chasing Eskimo families, demanding that they sell him their fox pelts—and even threatening to shoot the Eskimos' dogs if they refused. (Although in both these cases, the Eskimos believed they were doing the absolutely correct thing—protecting the welfare of their community—the government of Canada believed otherwise, and sentenced the killers to life imprisonment.)

The Ultimate Sacrifice

Lives were taken for the good of the community under other circumstances, as well. Sometimes during an especially brutal winter, when hunting was poor and families were starving, some Eskimo groups practiced the custom of infanticide—the systematic killing of certain newborns. It was not a common thing, but it was done.

Under Eskimo law, the killing of a newborn could not be viewed as murder if the baby had not been named. Almost without exception, the babies killed were little girls. Baby boys would grow up to be providers of food, the Eskimos reasoned, and unless they were weak and sickly, the boys were allowed to live.

Without discussion, the father of a doomed newborn girl would suffocate her quickly, or take her outside and put her in a snowbank, where she would die within a few minutes. And like the other instances of killing in Eskimo society, such infanticide was viewed as an essential act in a community whose survival was at stake. One less mouth to feed would certainly help.

In addition, there have been many instances in traditional Eskimo society of old people committing suicide so that they would not be a burden to their families. A Danish explorer wrote that in some Inuit communities, an old man who was in deteriorating health would make a joyful celebration out of ending his life.

During especially brutal winters when food was scarce, the killing of newborns and the suicide of the elderly were sacrifices occasionally made for the good of the community.

He would call for a feast . . . for his family and friends, in order that they might laugh and talk, and share once more the stories from times past.

The sharing over, he would walk quietly with them to the shoreline or to the edge of the ice, and taking leave of his family and friends, he would ask his wife or his eldest son to help him into his kayak. This done, he would paddle proudly out to sea until he was quite certain that he was alone and unseen, and with a determined thrust of his paddle, capsize his kayak for the last time.[22]

But in times of starvation, there were no feasts or parties. Old people might simply "disappear" during a family's desperate wintertime move to find food. During such journeys, the old people would ride on the sled, with their children and grandchildren walking along beside. "No words were spoken," writes one historian. "There were no farewells. The old people quietly eased themselves off the [sled], and waited in the snow for the end."[23]

Death was not an easy choice, nor was the end of a life taken lightly in Eskimo society. Life was precious, for there were so many threats to survival. But Eskimos believed that if an elder of their community had decided to make such a sacrifice for the good of the group, that wish must be respected.

Early Marriage

Infanticide, and the suicide of the old, were the exceptions, however, not the rule. For the most part, the family unit was happy and strong. Eskimos married early—few girls were unmarried by the age of thirteen or fourteen; boys married at seventeen or

A young Alaskan Eskimo couple, ca. 1902. Eskimo marriages were sometimes arranged by in-laws, and typically occurred at an early age.

eighteen. In some communities, marriages were arranged by the future in-laws when their children were still babies.

There was no special ceremony to mark the occasion of marriage. Sometimes a boy who wished to marry a girl would simply move in with her in her parents' home. The two would get to know each other while the girl had the security and guidance of her mother, while at the same time she learned how to make a comfortable home. If after six months or a year the two were still compatible, they would build a house of their own and begin living together. That signified a marriage in the community.

It was foolish for young people to wait too long to marry, or to be too picky in choosing a spouse. They would not meet many eligible people during their lives—especially when one considers that the great majority of the members of a band were relatives! It was only by marrying and starting a family that the community would continue, and traditions and customs would remain alive.

The Most Loved

Most Eskimo families had only two or three children, although parents with larger families were considered very lucky. A high rate of infant mortality claimed many Eskimo children under the age of two. The fluctuating temperature and humidity inside sod houses was responsible for a great deal of illness among babies. "Igloos killed babies as if they were mosquitoes," writes one expert. "They were damp and cold, and a lot of babies died of pneumonia."[24]

Eskimos had fewer children for another reason. Eskimo mothers nursed their children years longer than women in most cultures, and the nursing had a natural contraceptive effect. Almost all children were nursed long past their toddler years; it was not uncommon for children as old as eight or ten to be nursed occasionally.

Children in traditional Eskimo families were highly valued and deeply loved. Both fathers and mothers were quick to cuddle a crying baby, and parents spent every evening holding and rocking their children. From infancy to about age two, an Eskimo baby was carried around inside the mother's fur parka all day. Children needed no clothing, for they were warmed by the heat of their mother's body. "Aside from being bounced around as her mother did her chores," one writer observes, "the only hardship a child faced was early toilet training—being yanked out of the warm parka into the chilly air and held naked over the snow."[25]

Stirring Them Up, and Special Names

Children were rarely scolded or punished by their parents. When a child misbehaved, or had a temper tantrum, Eskimo parents viewed it as "forgetting" rather than disobeying. Parents had more experience living, so it was their duty to remind their children every once in a while how to live correctly.

"We stir them up a little to live right," explains a modern Eskimo father who raises his children in a traditional way:

> [We] tell them to obey the parents. Do what people tell them to do. And like now, when they go on a camping trip, not to take a new pillow. It get dirty on the trip. Take old one. They young. They don't know what to do. We tell them how to do things. Like our parents used to tell us. Same they used to talk to us. . . . Stir them up. They forget.[26]

Another reason Eskimo parents were unwilling to punish or scold their children had to do with their names. It has always been customary in Inuit and Yupik communities for babies to receive an *atiq*, or special

name. The name is usually that of a favorite relative or family friend who has just died.

Eskimos believe that when a baby receives his or her special name, the dead person's spirit enters the newborn. It makes no difference in Eskimo languages whether the name belonged to a man or woman, for Eskimo names have no gender distinctions. Therefore, in a single community, there might be several children—both boys and girls—named after a brave hunter or a wise grandmother.

And if it is believed that some of the spirit of that hunter or grandmother lives on in those children, it is difficult for parents to be harsh in raising them. "If I give my grandfather's *atiq* to my baby daughter," explains one

Traditional Eskimo parents were very loving and affectionate toward their children, and rarely punished them for misbehavior.

Inuit father, "she is my grandfather. . . . Can I scold her? Could I tell my grandfather he ought to be in bed? Could I instruct my grandfather to finish his breakfast?"[27]

Fun, but Not for Too Long

A small Eskimo child traditionally led a rather free existence. Children typically played, ate, and slept at whim. There were no strict schedules; parents believed that the child knew best when he was sleepy or needed food. Play was much like play in any group of children—Eskimo children enjoyed tag, hide-and-seek, and make-believe. They wrestled and laughed and played with the puppies. Eskimo fathers spent many evenings making dolls, animals, and tops for their young children.

But those days were short-lived. By the age of nine or ten, Eskimo children were expected to begin learning the work of their parents. Little girls used miniature sewing kits, and helped their mothers with weaving and sewing. In some communities they even used smaller versions of the *ulu*, the women's knife, to learn how to butcher and skin animals. Little boys played with small harpoons and bows and arrows, and talked longingly of being old enough to hunt with the men.

Each Eskimo group had special ways of integrating children into the adult community. When a little boy killed his first animal, his parents proudly announced the accomplishment by hosting a party. Even if the animal was only an insect, the child was hailed as a hunter. His mother proudly stuffed and kept all his first year's kills—mice, birds, whatever he brought home to her.

It was much the same for a young girl. When she first picked a berry, or spotted an egg in a nest, her parents bragged that she

Eskimo children gave up their carefree existence at the age of nine or ten to learn the work of their parents. Here, a young boy learns to hunt with a bow and arrow.

was becoming a woman, who soon would be cooking and feeding a family of her own. A party was held in her honor, and gifts were distributed to all the guests, to celebrate the occasion.

Knowing How to Have Fun

Parties celebrating their children's accomplishments were not the Eskimos' only occasions for having fun. One might think that the dismal, cold environment of the Arctic would snuff out any thoughts of having a good time, but it did not. Whether to mark a special event, or merely to pass the long days of winter when the sun did not shine, the Eskimos would celebrate their community by having a party.

Eskimo Dancing

In The Eskimos, *Ernest S. Burch Jr. describes the intricate system of dances done by traditional Eskimos. Some dances were done for ceremonial purposes, for entertainment, or simply to pass the time. The most interesting dance, according to Burch, probably was the wolf dance, which consisted of several stages, or episodes.*

"In the first, three or four women and two men danced. The women held wands or rods decorated with feathers, and they did their typical swaying dance on one side of the floor, while on the other side, the men, wearing loonskin head-dresses and long gauntlet mittens, performed a pantomime dance expressing a wish to go outside. The mittens, and often the head-dresses, also served as rattles, small stones or bones, or perhaps amulets encased in membranes, being attached to them. The orchestra of perhaps three men playing frame drums and one man playing box drums was seated to one side of the dance floor, and the audience was seated across from it. The fourth side of the dance floor was occupied by a screen symbolizing a wolf den.

The central episode began when a single male dancer wearing a wolf's head mask . . . performed a dance depicting the wolf character. Simultaneously, four similarly attired dancers enacted a complex series of maneuvers and contortions behind the partially opened wolf den. They then emerged to dance on the main floor. During this part of the performance they conveyed gifts between different members of the audience, dancing all the while. When the gift distribution had been accomplished, they leapt backward, in unison, through small holes in the 'den' wall. As they disappeared, their masks and mittens were scraped off onto the floor."

In many traditional Eskimo communities, families built tunnelways between their houses, to make it easier to get together; other Eskimo groups built a separate house, larger than the others, that was strictly used for get-togethers.

The activities included a great many games, most of which are played in Eskimo communities to this day. There were contests to see who could jump rope the longest, or in the most creative way. There was a game sometimes referred to as "two-kick," which required considerable athletic ability. Each player was supposed to jump up and strike an object with both feet simultaneously, and then land on the floor on two feet. Some Eskimo men could hit an object ten feet off the floor; the women's record seems to have been just over six feet.

One Yupik Eskimo recalls his grandparents playing a game with a top. "The idea was to set the thing spinning as hard as you can, because you had to dash out the door, run all the way around the house and come back in before the top stopped," he explained. "The way I understand it, the game was lots of fun for the people watching—sometimes they would clap in unison and yell to the one outside that the top was about to fall, just to watch him scoot as fast as he could."[28]

Eskimos loved to fill the long, cold Arctic days with parties and games. Like this game of tug-of-war, many traditional Eskimo games are still being played in Eskimo communities.

Drum dancing has always been a popular activity at Eskimo gatherings, too. Sometimes a single drummer, at other times several, would beat drums while others chanted a chorus. Others would move to the beat of the

Drum dancing is still a favorite at many Eskimo gatherings. Participants act out familiar and often humorous stories and events to the beat of one or more drummers.

drum, acting out familiar stories and events. Sometimes the dance depicted a dangerous or exciting hunt, or a journey the group had taken. But often the dance was comedic, meant to make the audience laugh—a dance showing a naughty child, or a hunter trying to control a team of crazy sled dogs.

Singing was a big part of the Eskimo community. As one historian writes, "Eskimos sang to pass the time of day. They sang while they worked and while they danced. They played games with songs. They ridiculed each other with songs. They quieted distraught children with songs. They performed magic with songs. And they sang songs as part of their songs."[29]

Many of the songs Eskimos sang were old—tunes they had heard their parents and grandparents sing years before. But many Eskimos made up their own songs, too, and taught them to others in the community. In the 1920s a Danish explorer was astounded at the number of different songs he heard in the village each day. He asked one of the Eskimos how many songs he himself had composed. The man couldn't estimate. He

The Storyknife

One of the favorite pastimes for young Eskimo girls used to be storytelling, with the help of a special knife, called a storyknife. The activity is described in Inua: Spirit World of the Bering Sea Eskimo, *edited by William W. Fitzhugh and Susan A. Kaplan.*

"Perhaps the most interesting . . . pastime is that spent by Bering Sea Eskimo girls who tell one another stories while illustrating them in the mud . . . with the aid of story-knives. A storyknife is a knife-shaped implement usually made out of ivory, but sometimes fashioned out of antler or wood. The knife, made for a little girl by her father, has a handle carved in the form of a fish or bird seen in profile. . . .

Little girls have favorite places where they gather to tell stories. These spots may be chosen because the mud is an unusual red or has lovely multicolored stripes running through it. Using the tip of her knife, a little girl will draw an opening scene in the mud defining the space in which the story is taking place. She draws people, furniture, bushes, and mountains as they appear during the progress of the story. . . . The stories cover a number of topics including myths, adventures, ghosts, and there is a class of stories that teach moral values. This last category is quite common, and usually features a child who disobeys her mother's or grandmother's instructions and brings misfortune to a relative. The strongest messages in these stories relate to how the disobedient child has risked her own life and has endangered the entire community because of her misdeeds."

told the explorer, "I merely know that I have many, and that everything in me is song. I sing as I draw breath."[30]

Storytelling was a popular Eskimo pastime, and like singing, it was an important way of maintaining the culture. The elders of the community were usually the most skilled storytellers—they made even the most often-repeated stories exciting by adding new details or special sound effects. Youngsters in the community were often encouraged to memorize the stories, for they would some-day be the storytellers. Because Eskimos had no written language, the oral tradition was vital to keeping the link between present and past.

But as tight as these Eskimo communities were, and as successful as they have been at keeping their traditions alive, events have taken place in the Arctic and subarctic during the past several decades that have rocked those traditions to their foundation. What sort of threat could have challenged such a tightly knit culture?

The Coming of the Outsiders

Although the most drastic change in Eskimo tradition has taken place since about 1950, the culture was threatened long before. Some hints of impending troubles appeared as early as the sixteenth century, when the first explorers from Europe came to the Arctic.

Kidnapped

Many of the explorers were looking for what they called the Northwest Passage, an all-water route to Asia. In 1577 Sir Martin Frobisher, an Englishman sailing to the Far North in eastern Canada, spotted a few Inuit hunters in kayaks. Shocked to find humans living in such a cold and desolate land, Frobisher seized upon the idea of capturing the hunters as proof of the strange things he had seen on the journey.

Hoping to lure the men to the ship, Frobisher began ringing a bell. The Eskimos were fascinated; metal was unknown to them, so of course they had never seen a bell. One of the hunters came close to the ship, and when he did, Frobisher's men grabbed him—kayak and all. The poor Eskimo was taken back to England, where he was presented to Queen Elizabeth I as "an oddity of the far North."

The queen was delighted with the Inuit, and amused the lords and ladies of the court by forcing the hunter to demonstrate his hunting ability. She particularly enjoyed having him harpoon her swans in the Royal Garden. (Sadly, the hunter did not survive long in England; cut off from the support of his family and community, he became lonely and died of a cold.)

In 1577 Sir Martin Frobisher captured an Inuit hunter and brought him back to England. There, the Eskimo was presented as "an oddity of the far North" to Queen Elizabeth I, who forced him to demonstrate his hunting ability for the amusement of the court.

The profitable whaling industry brought European whalers to the Arctic in droves during the eighteenth and nineteenth centuries.

"Like Brute Beasts"

Unfortunately for the Inuit, more explorers followed Frobisher. Not every contact with these outsiders was as humiliating as the first, but a reading of the journals kept by many of these explorers makes it clear that the Eskimos were treated as much as oddities as they appeared to Frobisher. Many explorers believed the Eskimos were no better than savages or beasts. "They eat their meat all raw," wrote one visitor to the Arctic in 1589, "both flesh, fish, and fowl, or something boiled with blood and a little water which they drink." Also, remarked the visitor, "the Eskimos pluck up [wild vegetation] and [would] eat . . . like brute beasts devouring the same."

The Eskimos' lack of table manners—or tables, for that matter—disgusted the same visitor. "They neither use table, stool, or table cloth . . . but when they are imbrued with blood knuckle deep, and their knives in like sort, they use their tongues as apt instruments to lick them clean."

And the sod houses of the Eskimos were judged as no more than horrible smelling animal caves. "Their winter dwellings . . . are made two fathoms underground . . . having holes like to a fox. . . . They defile these dens most filthily with their beastly feeding, and dwell so long in a place . . . until their sluttishness loathing them, they are forced to seek a sweeter air."[31]

The Whalers Arrive

Although the explorers were narrow-minded in their arrogance, they did nothing to harm the Eskimos' way of life. The explorers made detailed maps of the Arctic, however, and this activity *did* prove harmful. Guided by such maps, more and more ships from Europe cruised the Arctic region. And while the explorers did not find the elusive water route to Asia, they did notice that the cold Arctic seas were brimming with whales. And that meant there was a lot of money to be made.

Relations between Eskimos and European whalers at first seemed promising: Eskimos traded pelts and seal meat for useful tools, and whalers benefited from the Eskimos' exceptional harpooning skills.

Whales were increasingly in demand in Europe. In the eighteenth and nineteenth centuries, whale oil was used for street lamps. Whale tongue was a delicacy, much sought by the royalty of Europe. And *baleen*, the hornlike material in the upper jaw of a whale, which allows the animal to filter its food from seawater, was used for all sorts of things—from women's corsets, to umbrella ribs, to high-priced furniture. Whaling was so profitable, in fact, that a whaling ship could bankroll its entire expedition by killing only one or two whales.

The Eskimos at first welcomed the whalers. Their tradition taught them that the oceans were not owned by anyone, and that whoever needed whales should hunt them. Some good relationships developed between Eskimos and whalers. The captains frequently hired Eskimos to work on the ships, and although the new recruits had difficulty communicating with the Europeans, their skill at harpooning the great whales was priceless. Eskimos and Europeans also traded goods— the Eskimos were pleased to exchange fur pelts and seal meat for mosquito netting, mirrors, metal knives, and needles.

Unwelcome Gifts

But the whaling ships brought very unpleasant things, too—things that were very harmful to the Eskimos' traditional way of life. As one writer explains, "These rough seafarers were intent exclusively on plundering the seas and exploiting the local inhabitants, whom they treated with contempt. Money was their only interest."[32]

For example, there had been no alcohol in Eskimo communities until the whalers not only "showed the Inuit how to use tobacco, [but also] gave them whiskey, and taught them how to distill spirits from molasses and potatoes, which they traded for slippers and

A seal-shaped Eskimo tobacco pipe, carved from an ivory walrus tusk. Tobacco smoking caught on quickly after its introduction to the Eskimos by European whalers.

tobacco pouches of seal skin."[33] Alcoholism and the violence it often creates then became a terrible problem. Often, say historians, whalers got Eskimos drunk simply for their own amusement, laughing as a man became disoriented and clumsy.

And as some Eskimos found out, drunkenness could have more deadly consequences. "It was not uncommon for an [Eskimo], awakening from a drunken stupor the next morning, to find himself on the deck of a whaler bound for Holland," writes one historian, "where he was sold to a travelling showman and exhibited at fairgrounds across Europe. Kidnapping became increasingly common, and many families deprived of a hunter were left to die."[34]

The whalers brought more subtle evils, too. Germs and viruses to which the Eskimos had never been exposed (and to which their immune systems offered no defense) spread quickly from the whalers to the Eskimos. Eskimos died by the thousands from diseases such as measles, tuberculosis, smallpox, and influenza. Some historians estimate that the Eskimo population was reduced by 80 percent by these diseases.

In Alaska, says one writer, the Yupik Eskimos "fell like blighted grass" to smallpox.[35] Whole villages were wiped out. In some communities plagues of measles were so deadly that those who survived the disease were left too weak to hunt, and soon died of starvation. In many communities the disease sped from house to house so quickly that there was no time to bury the dead. Writes one expert, "Corpses piled up in the . . . sod houses and in the spring starving dogs ate the bodies of their masters."[36]

A Trail of Death

The Eskimos' environment changed dramatically as well. Many species of whales were hunted almost to the point of extinction. When one species seemed to disappear, however, the whalers began hunting a different

Tuberculosis in the Eskimo Village

Eskimos who were found to have tuberculosis (TB) were sent away from the village to a special treatment and recuperation center for TB victims called a sanatorium. The event was wrenching for patients and families alike, as James Houston told reporter Mary D. Kierstead for her New Yorker *article, "The Man: A Profile of James Houston."*

"And then there was TB. If a mother had a positive x-ray, we would tell her that she had to go out on the icebreaker to one of the distant sanatoriums. There were some sad scenes on the beach when the icebreaker was about to leave. To the Eskimos, a woman was neither alive nor dead when she was away. Of course, some women returned, but some babies were lost. A child [who had been sent away with TB] would come back into the country years later no longer speaking Inuktitut, and no one would know who the parents were, or even which part of the Arctic he came from. 'Anyone short a little boy?'"

A British whaling ship in 1905, surrounded by corpses of dead whales. Whalers hunted the huge beasts almost to the point of extinction, forcing Eskimos to rely on other animals for food and fuel.

one. Many Eskimos, who depended on whales for survival, were forced to look to other animals for food and fuel.

"Like Cattle Lying in a Barnyard"

When whales were scarce, the whaling ships began killing other sea animals—especially walruses. Their fat contained oil that could be used as fuel, and their tough, inch-thick hide was useful for tarpaulins and—in the early twentieth century—bicycle seats. Most appealing about the walrus, however, were the long ivory tusks, which were valuable for making combs, brushes, and decorative items.

The whalers did to the walruses what they had done to the whales—except in a much bloodier way. While the large animals sunned themselves on ice floes, hunters fired at them with rifles. The ease with which the

killing was done horrified some witnesses, who described the walruses as being "like cattle lying in a barnyard."

An Eskimo man makes a harpoon from the long ivory tusk of a walrus. Walruses were valuable to the Eskimos not only for their tusks, but also for their meat, hide, and fat.

So unsuspecting were the animals that the whalers could kill hundreds at a time by firing into a sleeping herd. "There were times when the heat of the blood spilling from butchered walruses ate through the ice floes," one writer reports, "dumping an entire catch into the sea."[37]

European ships slaughtered the walruses by the tens of thousands. It is estimated that more than four million were killed altogether. And, just as in the case of the whales, the Eskimos felt the loss in their own communities. Many Eskimo hunters found that they could paddle in their kayaks for days and never see a walrus. One animal could have fed the community for weeks, but none were to be found.

Widespread hunger was the result. Eskimo communities that relied on whale and walrus meat were starving. Many villages butchered their sled dogs out of desperation, and when those were dead and eaten, they ate mice, seaweed, and even boiled their fish-skin boots to make a watery, sour soup.

From Whalers to Fur Traders

As unexpectedly as they had arrived, the whaling ships left and never returned. Commercial whaling was pretty much over by the beginning of the twentieth century, for there was little money in it. Petroleum had made whale oil unnecessary; plastics had replaced baleen. Because the whale and walrus population had been decimated, whaling expeditions could no longer make a profit.

The departure of the whalers did not mean an end to European involvement in the Arctic, however. Traders of animal pelts had been operating for years in Eskimo territory, and as the whaling industry floundered, the

Seal Hunting in Warm Weather

In The Eskimos *Ernest Burch Jr. explains how hunting styles varied from season to season. Especially interesting was the hunting of seals in warm weather, when the animals sunned themselves on the ice.*

"In the spring, when the sun starts to appear again in the north, seals crawl out on the ice to warm themselves in its rays. They lie right beside the hole or crack from which they emerged, raising their heads every minute or so to look around for danger. The only way a hunter can approach a sunning seal is to stalk it by crawling over the ice on his stomach, pretending to be another seal. When his intended quarry's head is down, the hunter inches forward, often through pools of frigid water if the spring thaw has commenced. When the seal raises its head, [the hunter] either lies absolutely still, acting like a sleeping seal, or else he also raises his head and looks around, attempting to simulate the motions of a seal. Fortunately for Eskimo hunters, a seal's eyesight is not particularly good. A stalk might require several hours when carried out on flat ice, however, and there is never any guarantee that the quarry will wait that long. Eventually, if the hunter is lucky, he will approach within a few meters of his quarry and strike it with his harpoon."

fur business thrived. Throughout the world, fur was prized as a mark of success and wealth. Fox, mink, seal, polar bear—all were in great demand, and the more pelts the traders could supply, the better.

The fur traders depended on the Eskimos more than the whalers had. Eskimos knew how to brave the weather and how to track animals in the frozen desert. Every pelt the Eskimos could supply was eagerly bought by the traders. No money was needed, for the well-stocked trading stores had an abundance of items the Eskimos wanted—metal cooking pots, flour, tobacco, and matches.

Mass-Kill Tools

But the most sought-after item in the trading store was a rifle. Ironically, rifles did more to erode the traditional Eskimo way of life than any other single European intervention. At first, the benefits from the use of this weapon seemed enormous. Here, after all, was a tool that would make hunting easier and safer. Eskimo women and children would no longer have to rush at caribou herds, for example, startling them so that they would run toward the men, poised and ready with spears and bows and arrows. An Eskimo hunter had only to point and shoot—he did not even need to get close. Hunting with a rifle took far less skill than shooting a bow and arrow. To a people for whom starvation was a real and constant threat, the rifle must have seemed like the most wonderful gift of all.

The traders urged the Eskimos to try another tool—steel traps. Eskimos were no strangers to traps, but the ones they had used for centuries were made of rocks, bone, or even ice. The sharp steel traps were far more effective. Besides, they didn't need to be rebuilt each time, nor was it necessary to

While rifles and steel traps eliminated starvation, they also played a large role in the erosion of the Eskimo way of life.

worry about them melting! It seemed that with such tools, the Eskimos would soon be a very prosperous, well-fed people.

Eroding the Traditions

But the advantages of rifles and steel traps were short-lived. The rifles enabled the Eskimos to shoot far more game than ever before; but the numbers of animals decreased more quickly. More animals were killed than necessary—the old tradition of killing only what was needed was abandoned. Killing animals not really needed for food or clothing, while earning the Eskimos a good living at the trading store, endangered the future livelihood of the community.

Some Eskimo communities understood the consequences of abandoning the old weapons very quickly. The bows and arrows might have been clumsy and slow, but they had been quiet. Eskimo hunters were finding that the loud bangs of the rifle were frightening the animals—particularly herds of caribou, which quickly changed their migration patterns away from the noisy hunters.

The steel traps were having their effect, too. The white fox, much in demand for coats by rich women all over the world, was at its peak in the winter months. Its coat was thickest and whitest then, so traders encouraged the Eskimos to set their traplines during the coldest months of the year.

But traditionally, winter had been a time for seal hunting. It was then that the Eskimos obtained their winter meat, as well as the skins that were so important for tents and clothing. Winter had also been a time for getting together with the community, for singing and listening to the stories that made up the cherished culture.

Instead of participating in community socializing and hunting for their families, however, many Eskimos now spent the dark winter days patrolling their traplines—sometimes hundreds of miles long. And the result was often catastrophic. As one writer reports, "Families were left without skins for clothes, boots, and tents, or winter seal meat, surviving on food purchased on credit from the trading post."[38]

A Vicious Cycle

And so the relationship between the outsiders and the Eskimos proved a vicious cycle. The hunters used the rifles and steel traps, then sold their catch to get credit at the

A trading post in Nome, Alaska, offers furs and Eskimo crafts for sale. With few animals left to hunt, the Eskimos increasingly relied on trade and money for survival.

store to buy more ammunition and more traps. As a result, the populations of game animals diminished, and Eskimos began to starve. As people grew hungrier, they needed the rifles even more, for there was no time to wait for days at a breathing hole for a chance to kill a seal.

The Eskimos' economy changed from one of subsistence—relying totally on themselves for all essentials—to one of money or trade. Unable to feed themselves on seal, whale, caribou, and walrus, the Eskimos were turning more and more to food purchased at the trading post. They were no longer self-reliant. Somehow, the outsiders had taken charge.

But no outside presence remained in the Eskimo territory for long. Like commercial whaling, the fur industry declined, and the traders left as quickly as the whalers had. The consequences of their departure were in some cases tragic, for the Eskimos had come to depend on the new way of life.

One Eskimo hunter recalled the departure of the fur traders from his territory in the 1920s:

I remember [one] winter well, for the traders told us they must have many foxes that year. They were so anxious that we gave up the great fall hunt of the [caribou] and used all our skill and our strength to trap foxes, believing we could trade them for food at the place of the white man. . . . But when, in midwinter, we took our pelts south, the door of the wooden igloo stood open and the white man had gone. . . . The boxes were empty and there was no food in the place and no shells for our guns, so we could not even hunt meat for ourselves.[39]

Due to the scarcity of many animal populations, Eskimos could no longer rely on hunting to supply food and clothing. This family was forced to buy cloth from a trading post to make clothing.

I Was Alone

In this poem Flora Nash, a young Yupik girl, reflects on the need for community. It is a theme very common among stories and songs in Eskimo tradition. This poem, in English and in Yupik, is included in the collection Through Yupik Eyes.

I was alone.
I felt like an island.
Nobody came,
Nobody talked,
Nobody comforted me.

Then life began.
When people came
They talked, laughed
And played with me.
But something was missing . . .

I wondered,
But found no answer.
I looked,
And still I found nothing.

Soon I know
I'll find the answer.

The same thing happened to other Eskimo communities as late as the 1940s. Without warning, their new way of life disappeared. No longer were they paid trappers—they were simply unemployed people, who all of a sudden had neither game to feed themselves as they once had, nor the income with which to buy food.

The situation did not improve as new outsiders came to Eskimo territories. During World War II, from 1939 to 1945, and the cold war with the Soviet Union that followed the hostilities in Europe and the Pacific, the Alaskan North became strategically important. Americans arrived to build and staff military bases. The Canadian Arctic became a new frontier for the petroleum and mining industries. Instead of whalers and fur traders, Eskimos were coming into contact with engineers, miners, and government officials—both Canadian and American.

And though some Eskimos no doubt were frustrated by this turn of events, each passing year has increased their dependence on the outsiders. The Real People have been pushed into the modern age, and in the process have had to pay the price—the loss of control over their lives.

"In Their Best Interests"

The history of relations between the Eskimos and outsiders has often been one of profiteering and exploitation. People like the whalers and traders were in the Arctic to make money, pure and simple. Their only interest in the Eskimos and the arctic environment lay in exploitation for personal gain.

But other outsiders have tried, or are currently trying, to help correct what seems to be wrong among the Eskimo people. Sometimes this "correcting" has made life better for the Eskimos; other times it has proven as harmful as the exploitation of the earlier visitors. In both cases, Eskimo villages today reflect the effort of these outsiders.

One of the first groups to "help" were the missionaries. They came from several denominations—Lutheran, Roman Catholic, Moravian, Presbyterian, and Quaker. Some journeyed to the Arctic as early as the eighteenth century; others continue their work even today. From the outset, their goal has been to save souls, to spread their respective versions of the word of God to people who had never had the opportunity to hear it.

A Christian missionary spreads the word of God to a group of Eskimos. Many early missionaries were appalled at the living and hygienic habits of the Eskimos, and dismissed their spiritual beliefs as nonsense.

The Cycle of Souls

In Eskimo Essays, Ann Fienup-Riordan explains the complex traditional beliefs of Yupik Eskimos about the animals they killed to survive. Most important among these animals is the seal, on whom they depended for meat, fuel, and skins for clothing.

"In the Yupik world, no one ever finally passes away out of existence. . . . This cycling of human souls is especially interesting when considered in light of the traditional belief that the souls of the seals must be cared for by the successful hunter in order that they, too, will be born again. Seals as well as other animals and fish are believed to give themselves to men voluntarily. A seal, for instance, is said to sense, and in fact to see, the merits of a hunter. If the hunter is seen to be 'awake' to the rules of the proper relationship between humans and animals, and between humans and humans, [the seal's] soul will stay alive and await return to the sea. In fact, traditionally, the coastal Yupik Eskimos held a Bladder Festival every winter. At the Bladder Festival the bladders of the seals caught during the year along with the bladders of other animals were inflated, hung at the back of the men's house, and feasted and entertained for five days. Then, on the fifth day, each family took the bladders of the animals they had killed to the sea and pushed them down through a hole in the ice so that the souls of the seals might be born again."

Shamans, Charms, and Seal Bladders

Even though they had no worship services or formal ceremonies, as found in most religions, the Eskimos were not without spiritual traditions. Their religion was an everyday system of beliefs, the most important of which was that all aspects of nature have a spirit, or soul. People, animals, even the seasons and the weather—all were endowed with individual spirits.

Such beliefs were important to hunters, who were thus obliged to respect and honor the animals they killed. For an animal's spirit to be reborn, it was crucial that the animal be honored in death. A hunter who killed a seal, for instance, always put a little water in the dead animal's mouth as a token of respect, to show that the seal's spirit would soon return to the water.

Interestingly, the Eskimos believed that the living spirit of many animals—including the seal—remained in the animal's bladder when it was killed. For that reason, the Eskimos did not eat seal bladders. They saved them for a celebration called the Bladder Festival, held in midwinter. After inflating the bladders like balloons, they sang songs and gave speeches to honor the seals they had killed that year. After the celebration, the bladders were released under the winter ice, where according to traditional Eskimo beliefs they would give birth to more seals.

Special people in Eskimo communities could channel their energy and communicate with spirits. These men or women, called shamans, could do both harm and good. They could influence hunting, and cure people or make them sick. Shamans were greatly feared in the community, for their ways were strange, and it was believed that they were not human. Even so, when the need in the community was great, the shamans were consulted.

"[People] don't bother the shaman too much," recalls one Eskimo. "But . . . [when people do need such help] when there are no animals, they pay one that has powerful shamanistic powers to perform their powers, to find out. That is how the shamans [worked] in those days."[40]

One man claims that in 1902 his father was killed by a shaman. The shaman, angry that the boy's father wouldn't get a divorce and marry his own daughter, was said to have worked evil magic with a piece of the man's garment. "My mother tells about it," says Waldo Bodfish, an Alaskan Eskimo. "[The shaman] took a piece of [my father's] parka, on the hem. He didn't know about it. He died, getting sick."[41]

Shamans were feared in the Eskimo community for their purported ability to communicate with the spirits. This carving depicts a shaman conjuring spirits during a seance.

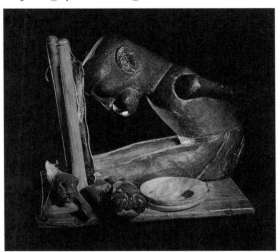

This human-shaped ivory amulet was once worn around the neck of an Eskimo as a charm to bring good luck.

But for good or evil, the shamans were not consulted for everyday troubles. Good luck with weather or hunting could be earned by good behavior, or by the use of special charms, called amulets. These were small ornaments worn on clothing, on necklaces, or in headbands. Some were made of bone and ivory, others were beaks of birds or the skulls of small animals.

"Everything to Learn . . ."

The missionaries who arrived in the Far North had little knowledge of the spiritual beliefs of the Eskimos. Their attitude was the same as that of many white people who had contacts with Eskimos or Native Americans—that native people had everything to learn when it came to Western religions—and absolutely nothing to offer. The shamans and the amulets they dismissed as hoaxes, the drums and sacred dances as mumbo-jumbo. None of it was, in the missionaries' eyes, *real* religion.

This attitude was extended to the Eskimo people as well as to their religion. The educated missionaries who had come from America and Europe were astonished at the living conditions in the Arctic, and taken aback by the culture that seemed so alien. Many of the missionaries admitted that they found it almost impossible to spread the word of God to people whose habits were so different from their own.

The lack of cleanliness was especially troubling to the missionaries. Many Eskimos had lice in their hair and clothing, for example. One missionary group near Bethel, Alaska, was so bothered by the lice on the Eskimos who came to visit that they actually debated whether to allow the prospective converts indoors. They finally decided, in a formal meeting, "that Christian charity . . . made it essential to entertain everyone, despite the lice they might bring with them."[42]

Another missionary was offended when the Yupik Eskimos she was trying to convert kept spitting tobacco juice on the floor of her cabin. She was even more shocked, she later reported, when after she had asked the men not to spit, "one man spit in his boot and another spit in his hand and rubbed the juice in his hair."[43]

Getting the Point Across

Cleanliness and hygiene aside, the first thing the missionaries tried to accomplish was to discredit the Eskimos' long-standing beliefs. The shamans were challenged and ridiculed by the missionaries as charlatans and tricksters. This enraged many shamans, who threatened the missionaries with curses and magic spells; but when nothing came of these threats, the missionaries won some converts.

The missionaries told the Eskimos that believing in magic spells or shamanistic powers was foolish. They forbade the women to wear charms to ensure safe childbirth, and the men were not allowed their amulets, which were believed to bring luck in hunting. From now on, the missionaries told the Eskimos, their faith must be in God's word, not magic.

Many Eskimos were willing to give Christianity a chance, for it seemed that the missionaries were powerful people. "To the Inuit," writes one historian, "Christian services such as baptism and communion were clearly rituals designed to assuage the spirits. The Bible was thought to be a magical device used for protection against hunger and disease. The missionary was undeniably a powerful [shaman] to be feared."[44]

An Inuit reads the Bible, which some Eskimos believed to be a magical device used for protection against hunger and disease.

One of the aspects of Eskimo tradition that was most bothersome to the Christian missionaries who came to the Arctic was the strong belief in the spirits of wind, water, and animals. In Women of Crisis: Lives of Struggle and Hope, *Robert Coles and Jane Hallowell Coles record an interview with an Eskimo woman named Lorna, who told about her grandmother's beliefs in such spirits.*

"The first memory I have is of my grandmother's hand. She was holding my hand. I remember feeling the squeeze. I remember seeing the lines on her hand, and noticing how smooth my hand was. I remember the pressure when she wanted me to stop or move or be silent and listen—listen to the wind. She would tell me she was about to leave us; she believed that one day a strong wind would come up—sent by the ice floes—and she would be standing near the water, and she would know that it was time; and the next thing, her spirit would say its last good-bye and speed across the land toward the mountains, far away. But she stayed with us a few years after she first told me that.

I remember being old enough to go to school, and hearing her tell me to pay attention because the wind was coming. She was always a step or two ahead of the wind. She kept her eyes moving and her ears wide open. 'Listen to the wind today,' she would say. Then she might tell us about the wind: 'It is someone's spirit—a very strong one, full of messages. Best to be quiet and learn.' I wouldn't dare open my mouth. I would stand and feel the wind coming toward me, then past me. Sometimes it would hit me, and I would try to hide behind my grandmother. She would try to get me to stand my ground, and not use her for protection."

Theological Questions

But certain aspects of the missionaries and their religion distressed the Eskimos. For one thing, these outsiders bringing the white culture's God were incredibly loud. The Eskimos almost always spoke in quiet voices; the voices of the missionaries were usually booming, especially when they delivered their sermons. The Yupik Eskimos called the missionaries who came to live among them the People of Thunder.

In addition, the rules the missionaries introduced about what was and was not allowed in their religion reflected ignorance of Eskimo culture. For instance, in traditional Eskimo society it was perfectly acceptable to take meat from another's supply if one needed food. Such an act was not considered stealing—for no one in the community was supposed to go hungry. But to the missionaries, taking meat from another without permission was indeed stealing. And thieves, they warned, would go to hell for eternity.

The idea of "Sunday" was foreign to the Eskimos, too. Their year was marked by the passage of seasons of the year, not weeks or days. But the missionaries believed that God had to be worshiped on the Sabbath, so the Eskimos began using special calendars—blocks of wood with seven holes into which they could fit a movable wooden peg. Not only were the Eskimos to make certain they attended church each Sunday, but they were forbidden to work on the seventh day, since the Sabbath was a day of rest.

The six-day week presented a problem for the Eskimos, who had no organized rest. They were used to resting when they needed to, not when a peg was moved to a certain hole in a wooden block. As one Eskimo expert asks, "What would happen . . . if after a period of blizzards and poor hunting, the first fair weather fell on a Sunday, and the seals were sunning themselves on the ice? Was hunting in such circumstances an infringement of God's law?"[45]

The missionaries' use of physical punishments was also troubling—and commonplace. One missionary in an Inuit settlement in Greenland wrote in his journal that disobedient Eskimos, those who refused to give up

The missionaries were successful in converting many Eskimos to Christianity. Churches are now common in many Eskimo villages.

their amulets and drum dances, were beaten. "I had to give him a few blows across the back," he wrote of his treatment of one strong-willed Eskimo hunter, "for nothing can make them see reason except beating and punishment, which I have to practice occasionally, having found that this worked."[46]

Sometimes such treatment was even part of religious education. One missionary tried desperately to make the Eskimos in his congregation understand the concept of evil. "He drew pictures of the Devil and punched the nearest Inuk [Eskimo] in the face to show that Satan was to be feared," reports one writer, "a tactic which succeeded only in frightening the . . . Inuit."[47]

New Prayers, Born-Again Puppies

Not every contact with the missionaries was violent, nor were the Eskimos patronized by everyone. Some tried very hard to be flexible and broad-minded in their instruction of the Eskimos. One missionary realized soon after he began his religious teachings that he would have to compromise if his lessons were to have any impact at all. According to Eskimo historian Sam Hall, the missionary was asked by the Inuits about the meaning of "daily bread" in the Lord's Prayer:

> "What is this daily bread that is so important that you must ask the [white man's] God for it every day?" The missionary responded with the amended translation "Give us this day that which tastes good," but the Inuits were still not satisfied. "Are there no seals in your heaven?" they asked. Eventually [the missionary] capitulated, changing the translation to "Give us this day the seal meat we need."[48]

There were other compromises, too. In some Eskimo communities the people were eager to be baptized, since the ritual seemed to carry so much importance. But why only people, they wondered? Their sled dogs, for example, were important in the community—vital to winter hunting. Why were they not included in the ritual? Surely they needed blessing and good luck as much as the Eskimos themselves. Some missionaries found it was easier to give in than to argue, so many puppies were baptized along with their masters.

Establishing Schools

The missionaries also started the first schools for Eskimo children during the 1940s and 1950s, to teach basic skills in reading and arithmetic. The missionaries felt that if the Eskimos were competent in these areas, they could more easily learn the important religious lessons.

The goal in Eskimo education—according to the schools—was assimilation. If only Eskimos could be more like whites, the schools reasoned, they would be better equipped for life in modern society. Even though the Eskimos knew very few English words, for example, all lessons in school were conducted in English. A few lessons at the beginning of the term were taught with an interpreter translating for the children, and after that they were on their own.

In addition, the missionaries forbade children to use their own language, and this frightened and frustrated Eskimo children. Many Eskimo adults today have painful memories of such schooling. "We quickly learned not to speak our own language in the classroom," remembers Inuit Ann Meekitjuk Hanson. "When we did, our hands were

A young Eskimo girl receives writing instruction from a Catholic priest. The first schools for Eskimos were started by missionaries in the 1940s and 1950s.

slapped with a wooden ruler. I remember being very silent. I would look into the eyes of my classmates and know what they were thinking. Silently we were saying, 'I wish we could speak.' We could not speak English because we had not learned it; we could not speak Inuktitut because it was forbidden. . . . We stayed silent. Only our eyes communicated."[49]

There were far more Eskimo settlements than there were missionaries, so schools were established only in the larger communities in Alaska and Canada. Eskimo parents were strongly encouraged to send their children to board at the schools, and a great number of parents did so, although they were skeptical about the value of a white man's education in the Arctic.

As a matter of fact, many parents worried about being separated from their children—at the time in their lives when they most needed guidance from their parents, children were far from home. How could they learn Eskimo ways? How could the family remain strong? "Our son, the son we loved best of all—we wanted to say no, he isn't going to your school," remembers one Inuit man. "He was so small, so young. We wanted to refuse. But we said yes. We were intimidated."[50]

Becoming "Civilized"

The missionaries believed they were improving these children's lives. If the Eskimo child were removed from the home environment, they reasoned, new ways could be more easily taught. As one expert writes of the missionaries in the Canadian Arctic, "[they] believed that the Inuit child would make better progress if placed in the proper environment of boarding school or private, non-native home."[51]

So Yupik and Eskimo children were airlifted out of their communities and sent to live in boarding schools in other villages, sometimes staying with white families near the school. Eskimo boys and girls who wanted to attend high schools were flown farther away at first—often to Bureau of Indian Affairs schools in Oklahoma or Oregon.

It is not surprising that a great many of these children were miserable and homesick. They were cut off from the only support system they had ever had, in a new environment that was different in every way from anything they had ever experienced. As one writer says, "Inuit children raised on seal and caribou meat were taught that a 'balanced diet' included fruits such as oranges—exotic fare in the Arctic. At school they ate with knives and forks, slept between sheets, and lived in plain but warm rooms."[52]

But even faced with massive culture shock, many Eskimo children did well at the boarding schools, where they learned English and arithmetic. They also became exposed to white culture. It is little wonder, then, that many of these children returned to their communities with uncomfortable new emotions. Compared to boarding school and the nonnative families they had met there, the parka-clad parents hunting and fishing for food seemed foolish. Children viewed their parents and the home they had grown up in with embarrassment. Even though they had not entered the white world, they were unwilling to go back to the traditional ways of their parents—as one writer puts it, "ashamed of their old world, but not ready for the new one."[53]

Even the language became a problem. Children who spent most of the year speaking English were coming home unable (and sometimes unwilling) to communicate with their parents and grandparents, who knew very little English. For the Eskimos, who had always depended on a strong oral tradition to keep the details of their culture alive from one generation to the next, the loss of a common language in the community was a disaster.

New Problems

Schools became government responsibilities in the 1960s, although mission schools still operate in parts of Canada and Alaska today. The governments of the United States and Canada, able to spend more money than was available to the missionaries, have established elementary schools in most communities. Younger children no longer are taken far from home to attend grade school, although few Eskimo communities have high schools.

But even with increased funding, Eskimo schools have been difficult to maintain. One problem has been the nomadic lifestyle of the Eskimo people. Although they are far more stationary than they once were, many communities "disappear" for months to hunt or fish. Children who leave before finishing a grade often have to repeat the following year, which is frustrating for students and teachers alike.

Another frustration is the difficulty in finding teachers. Until very recently, almost none of the teachers in the Arctic have been Eskimos. Most come from the "lower 48" or southern Canada. But good teachers are difficult to lure to the Arctic, for a variety of reasons. "The isolation, the climate, the barren, treeless environment made recruitment . . . difficult," writes one expert in Eskimo affairs. "When [teachers] were attracted to a settlement, they rarely stayed more than two years, and many stayed for only one year. In some cases teachers actually refused to leave the aircraft when it touched down at the isolated settlement."[54]

Alleviating Poverty

But education—or lack of it—has not been the only concern of the outsiders who have come to the Arctic. Poverty and starvation have been ongoing problems among the Eskimos, and both the United States and Canada have tried to alleviate them. As with education, some of the methods used in dealing with poverty and starvation have been criticized.

To American military people, and to Canadian miners and civil engineers newly arrived in the Arctic in the years following World War II, the conditions of the Eskimos were appalling. American soldiers stationed in Alaska reported whole villages of Yupik Eskimos living in poverty; Canadians found the same situation in their country with the Inuit and Inupiat. To typical citizens of the highly prosperous nations of Canada and the United States, it was inconceivable that their countries should contain villages of people virtually starving to death, people whose life depended on the dwindling herds

The governments of the United States and Canada took over responsibility for most Eskimo schools in the 1960s. Maintaining schools in these communities has not been an easy task.

One problem in Eskimo schools has been the lack of good teachers. The cold and isolation of the Arctic makes it difficult to lure qualified teachers from the lower 48 states.

of caribou and walrus. And so both governments took control of the populations of Eskimos within their borders. They urged Eskimos to settle in established communities, to end the migrations that had always been part of their existence. In fixed communities, the Eskimos could be near health care facilities and schools.

A great majority of Eskimos agreed to move to villages. It was becoming too difficult to live without the caribou, and, with the fur market in decline, they were not making much money trapping. It would be better to live where there were stores that sold food and clothing. The land was not providing them with much of either.

But money was surely a problem. There were few well-paying jobs in the Arctic, and those were held by the whites. Eskimos were hired to do menial work in the building of the oil pipelines, or in the construction of military bases. The money was good, but the jobs were temporary. When the pipelines were in place and the military bases finished, the work ended. Welfare and Social Security payments are the only income for most Eskimos.

Warps, Creaks, and Leaks

As attractive as village life seemed at first, Eskimos have had a hard time getting used to their new, permanent communities. The houses most Eskimos live in today, in fact, do not resemble the traditional sod houses most of them grew up in. Instead, most Eskimos

The Army Comes to the Arctic

In The Fourth World: The Heritage of the Arctic and Its Destruction, *Sam Hall describes the coming of the army to the Arctic in the 1950s. The military mission was to begin work on the Distant Early Warning system, or DEW line, a system of radar stations that would alert North America to the early stages of a nuclear attack by the Soviets.*

"The convoys and aircraft dumped hordes of fresh-faced men and countless tons of cargo barely a harpoon's cast from [the Eskimos'] traditional hunting grounds and houses of turf and stone. Intrigued, excited and bewildered, the Inuit stood by their dog teams and watched the intruders drive heavy trucks and bulldozers down the ramps. Innumerable sheets of corrugated iron were unloaded. In a single day the strangers bolted them together to create a city of tunnel-shaped huts and hangars. Soon soldiers had flattened a 10,000-foot runway along the valley. More aircraft circled overhead, and on landing disgorged drums of fuel and crates of food, which were stockpiled in the unloading bays, a store greater than the impoverished Inuit had seen, or heard of, in a lifetime. White radar domes, like giant golf balls, took shape, followed by a radar scanner so huge that it was likened to a football [field] tipped on its side.

In two years, 20,000 men passed through [the site], which grew into one of the biggest air bases in the world. The resident staff of 3,000 men carved tunnels in the ice, abandoned or burned trucks which failed to function in the cold, and littered the landscape with discarded packets of chewing gum and Camel cigarettes. Heaps of uneaten food were left for the foxes."

live in ordinary wooden homes much like those found elsewhere in North America. This change was orchestrated by the government employees who oversaw the establishment of the new villages.

Told repeatedly by health workers and visitors to the Arctic that traditional native houses were smelly, damp, and otherwise unhealthy, the governments of Canada and the United States urged the Eskimos to stop building sod homes (and in some cases snow houses). To make new homes affordable to a population that was almost totally without jobs, the governments made available low-interest loans and housing grants.

Building wooden houses in the Arctic is very difficult, for permafrost, the frozen layer of subsoil and rock which never thaws, lies right below the surface of the ground. In warmer climates builders dig foundations on which to construct a house, but in the Arctic such techniques are difficult and expensive. And building directly on the permafrost is foolish, for heat escaping from the bottom of the house will begin to melt the permafrost, causing shifting and damage to the structure.

Instead, Eskimos' homes are built either on gravel pads, which insulate the homes from the permafrost, or on stilts, three feet above the permafrost. The wood houses come in prefabricated kits, which are shipped by barge during the summer months, before ice makes boat travel impossible. The houses are painted at first, but the paint quickly wears away, buffed from the wood by the wind and snow. Once this has happened, usually within a year, it is rare for a house to be repainted.

But lack of paint has been the least of the Eskimos' problems. The house-building kits shipped in from warmer climates were not designed with Arctic living in mind. Many have doors that open out, which makes getting outdoors very difficult in winter, when snow drifts pile up outside. In addition, since the stilts and gravel pads have not been sufficient to insulate the houses from the cold, the alternate freezing and thawing of the surfaces of buildings causes them to warp and twist. As novelist Carolyn Meyer puts it, "even the most carefully built houses have no square corners or level floors or doors that close properly."[55]

"Old Eskimo Houses Were Warm"

Inadequate insulation in the wooden houses allows ice to form between the inner and outer walls, and large picture windows are leaky and drafty all winter. The result has been heating bills that are astronomically high, even though many Eskimos complain about being chilly. "You can't get warm like you could in the old [sod] houses, that's what my father says all the time," says a young Yupik man. "He doesn't like the big rooms, and he says the cold wind comes right in from the floor to your feet. There wasn't that problem the way Eskimos used to build houses."[56]

Katie Tokeinna, also from Alaska, agrees. As an elder in her community, she had been one of the first on a waiting list for the new housing, but she is not satisfied. "Old Eskimo houses were warm. I've been cold ever since I moved into a white man's house."[57]

Permafrost, a permanently frozen layer below the earth's surface, requires that homes in the Arctic be built on gravel pads or three-foot stilts. Here, with stilts in place, workers begin construction on a new home.

Other Eskimos, however, find the space in the wooden homes a welcome relief from the cramped quarters of their childhoods. One woman comments, "Now, with seven kids, I don't think I'd ever want to live in an igloo again. The children have never lived in one, and the space of a house is important. Even three bedrooms are not enough for us now!"[58]

The layout of such prefabricated houses is pretty standard. Most are constructed as one large room, without inside doors or complete walls. Partial walls or dividers separate eating and sleeping areas, as well as a bathroom. Most houses face south, away from the wind, and have an unheated porch where families keep large appliances like a freezer (not plugged in) or a washing machine when not in use.

Though many villages were promised plumbing—and houses were built under the assumption that it would be installed—many Eskimo communities are without it. A five-gallon bucket, known as the "honey bucket," is filled with disinfectant and a little water. The contents of this makeshift toilet are emptied on the ice outside the house each day. Bathtubs, put in by the builders, are used mostly to store dirty clothes.

A Mix of Old and New

The villages are not homogeneous, however. Some of the poorest families still build sod houses. Other families use sod houses for storage or for cleaning fish and game. Most families could not afford the price of lumber to build a second wooden structure.

There are nicer houses, too—dwellings that one writer maintains "could be anywhere in North America . . . only the carvings of seals, walrus, and drum dancers on the mantelpiece and bookshelves serve as a reminder of the conditions outside."[59] These are homes with foundations dug by bulldozers and excavation equipment brought in by barge at a huge expense to the owners. These houses almost always belong to outsiders—usually government employees or teachers. These houses have washers and dryers, and chemical toilets like those in camping trailers.

One thing almost every house has—regardless of whether its occupants are white bureaucrats, teachers, or Eskimos on welfare—is television, its signals pulled in by huge white satellite dishes. "It seems really sad," says Doug Meeker, a teacher who has worked with Yupik Eskimos in Alaska.

Television has replaced traditional Eskimo activities in many households in the Far North. Virtually no home is without one.

Most Arctic hunters have replaced dogsleds with faster, engine-powered snowmobiles. These machines have had the negative effect of diminishing animal populations at a much faster rate than traditional hunting.

"There are villages that vote to spend money on cable TV before they want indoor plumbing. The priorities seem wrong."[60]

But the Eskimos of Canada and Alaska feel that television is their one link to the culture of their neighbors in North America, their way of knowing what goes on in the rest of the world. Unfortunately, television is used less as an educational tool than as a way of keeping track of what jeans are most fashionable, what cars are hottest (even though most villages don't have roads), and the most prestigious basketball shoes. There are more than twenty channels available in the Far North, bringing news from Detroit, ice hockey and basketball, and game shows like *The Price Is Right* into every home.

One Inuit woman describes the initial impact of television in the Arctic this way: "It was intriguing, it was entertaining. It replaced the normal activities that we had in the communities, like visiting, playing together, sharing meals, working together. The streets were deserted. And I don't know if the novelty of television has completely worn off in the North yet."[61]

"The Metal Dogsled"

A few places in the Arctic still rely on dogsleds for transportation on the winter ice. In most communities, however, the dogsled has been replaced by the snowmobile. One advantage is obvious—an engine-powered hunter can make faster time than one towed by dogs. In addition, dogs eat on a regular basis, while the snow machines are "fed" only when used. The snowmobile has become as much a fact of Arctic hunting as the rifle.

But like other aspects of the new technology that have come to the Arctic in recent years, the snowmobile has glaring disadvantages. For example, the machines have given hunters the same sort of edge over their prey as the rifle. Thus, keeping up with fast-moving animals like caribou is much easier. As a result, however, the populations of large deer are diminishing.

And in case of emergencies, admit some Eskimo hunters, dog teams were better. "I know my father would rather be with dogs than the machine in a storm," says an Alaskan Yupik. "He always says you can't

Despite high maintenance costs and a short life expectancy, snowmobiles have become the main mode of transportation in the Far North.

North America rely on automobiles. The life expectancy of a new machine is far shorter than one in less severe temperatures—the bitter cold can kill a battery in an hour. To prevent this, owners keep their vehicles running on cold days, and plug them into battery warmers at night. Costs of the gas, oil, and maintenance for a snowmobile run between $6,000 and $10,000 each year.

Finally, the coming of the snowmobiles to the Far North has brought with it a new phenomenon—the junkyard. "On the edge of every Arctic township," writes one traveler, "there is a snowmobile graveyard, a tangled heap of discarded machines, dumped because extreme temperatures split the vinyl seat coverings, and the winter snowdrifts ruin the engines and metalwork."[63]

Although tremendous change has occurred in the Eskimo communities in recent years, and although many have been made with good intentions, numerous Eskimos feel that they have lost more than they have gained. Bryan and Cherry Alexander, who studied the Eskimo situation in Canada, feel the people there have been cheated. "The Inuit have been seduced," they write. "No more starvation, houses where heat and light came with the flick of a switch, medical facilities and schooling for their children. . . ."[64]

But what about the social aspects of Eskimo communities? Have the same clumsy attempts at assimilation affected the strong sense of community that has always marked the Eskimo culture?

snuggle up to a machine if you're cold, and dogs rarely break down. My grandfather says that a man he knows even ate two of his dogs when he was stranded on the ice for two weeks. I don't think there's a part of a snowmobile that I'd eat."[62]

Even so, a snowmobile or two is parked outside every house in most Eskimo communities, and is relied on as most people in

Day to Day:
Life in the Community

One of the biggest changes in the Eskimo lifestyle since the involvement of the outsiders has been the economy. By moving the Eskimos into permanent settlements, the U.S. and Canadian governments have made the traditional subsistence economy impossible. Unable to follow their grandparents' migrations in search of food, most Eskimos have become increasingly dependent on what they call *gussak* food—white man's food purchased at the community store.

No Good Deals

But store-bought food is extremely expensive. In 1990 a half-gallon of ice cream cost about $8, a box of crackers nearly $4. Soup goes for $2.50 a can—more than three times what it would cost in the lower 48. The non-food items are costly, too—more than $16 for a box of disposable diapers, and $10 for a box of laundry soap.

The reason for the high prices is simple. In the rest of Canada and the continental United States such products are shipped by truck. The Eskimo villages of the Arctic, however, are not served by roads. They can be reached only by barge (when the ice is broken up enough) and by airplane. These methods of transportation are very expensive, and are reflected in the prices of the goods brought into the villages.

The high price of food has not been its only drawback. Health officials say that while

fruits and vegetables are offered in the stores, the junk food is most popular. "During the past 30 years," writes one expert, "the Inuit have been introduced to potato crisps, gum, chocolate, white bread, hamburgers, hot dogs, and french fries swamped in ketchup and sweet mustard."[65]

The transition from a nomadic lifestyle to one of living in permanent settlements has made the Eskimos increasingly dependent on food purchased from community stores, usually at very high prices.

A Diet of Candy and Gum

The result of this enthusiastic consumption of junk food has been a high rate of nutritional deficiencies. Vitamins Eskimos used to get in seal meat and fish are not present in chewing gum and candy bars. One woman in Cape Dorset, a settlement in the eastern Arctic, reported that "people are beginning to depend upon bannock [fried bread], tea, soft drinks, candy, gum, and tinned [canned] foods for a diet." Also, she observed that "much food that is purchased here is merely eaten from the tin or package. Food value and nutrition are unheard of."[66]

Besides the obvious nutritional problems associated with a diet of candy and processed foods, there has been an epidemic of tooth decay—never before seen in Eskimo communities. The traditional diet of meat and fish was easy on teeth—in fact, skeletal remains many centuries old show Eskimos with cavity-free teeth. But with the *gussak* food came a 600 percent rise in sugar consumption, and with that, lots of cavities. Many Eskimos have teeth that are blackened and rotting, and it is not uncommon to see teenagers who have lost eight or ten teeth to decay.

Picking at Their Food

Not everyone likes *gussak* food—especially the nutritional varieties. Many schools in the Eskimo communities serve hot lunches to elementary students. The food is shipped from southern Canada or the United States, and by law must conform to nutritional standards set by the governments of those countries, but there are no raves for these meals, especially among children who are familiar with traditional Eskimo foods.

Novelist Carolyn Meyer depicts lunch at a typical school for Yupik Eskimo children:

> Old Mrs. Erickson scoops the food onto paper plates: chicken-noodle casserole, canned spinach, canned tomatoes, crackers, chocolate pudding, milk. . . . Mary picks dutifully at the food. The spinach does not taste at all like the wild greens her mother serves in early summer with salt and sea oil. She pokes the tomato experimentally and tastes some of the chicken-noodle dish. It's better than the vegetables, and she eats a little of it. Then she drinks all of her milk and finishes the pudding in no time.[67]

Many Eskimo parents worried when their children came home from school pale and hungry. Weren't they getting enough to eat? Couldn't the portions be larger? But the truth was, the *gussak* food was unfamiliar and often unpleasant to Eskimo children. And there seemed no real chance of inducing the government to serve the Eskimos seal meat or dried fish.

The popularity of processed junk foods in Eskimo communities has resulted in an epidemic of tooth decay—a problem never experienced with the traditional Eskimo diet.

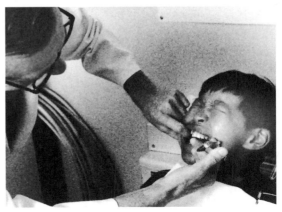

"Stinky Heads" and Eskimo Ice Cream

More and more Eskimo families are realizing that relying on store-bought food makes very little sense, nutritionally or economically. By supplementing their diet with traditional Eskimo fare, called "country foods," they can save money and enjoy delicacies of both sorts. One writer describes the kinds of food eaten by a modern Yupik family as "whale meat, peanut butter sandwiches, Tang, dried fish, Rice Krispies, boiled ducks, whitefish, fried bread, [and] popcorn."[68]

Many Eskimos are acquiring a taste for *gussak* foods, but the country foods are the favorites in most families. Soup made of seal flipper, and boiled duck—complete with head and feet—are enjoyed in numerous homes. *Masu*, a dish made of roots preserved in seal oil, is common. Seal oil, in fact, remains a staple in most Eskimo families. It has a strong flavor and is used as a dip when fish is eaten—definitely an acquired taste, according to some visitors to Eskimo homes!

One of the most unusual country foods favored by Yupik Eskimos is known as "stinky heads": fish heads—usually salmon—that are buried in the soil to rot. Months later they are retrieved, bluish green and slimy; the Yupik Eskimos, especially children, relish them.

By far the favorite of all "country food" desserts is called *akutag*, or "Eskimo ice cream." Traditionally *akutag* was made by mixing chunks of caribou fat with seal oil, and adding fish. The mixture was sweetened with blackberries or raisins and a little sugar. Because caribou are not always available, however, Eskimo women make their *akutag* with Crisco instead of the fat.

While many of the tools have changed, Eskimo fathers still teach their sons many of the hunting methods used by their ancestors. These lessons can help children learn more about the traditions of their heritage.

The Value of Hunting

So because the welfare checks do not cover their needs, and because they enjoy the taste of country foods, many Eskimos hunt as their fathers and grandfathers did. But hunting is valuable today for another reason, equally important—it is a good way for parents to acquaint their children with the skills and values of their heritage, a heritage that has nearly vanished.

"Children are taught about hunting when we are young," says one Inupiat boy, "because there is a lot to learn. The things we need to know cannot be found in books. We gain knowledge by watching and listening and by trying things out for ourselves."[69]

Threats to a Hunting Culture

One recent occurrence that has damaged the ability of the Canadian Inuit to earn money by hunting has been the outcry against the killing of seals, especially baby harp seals, so valued by some of the world's people because of their snow-white coat. But as Bryan Alexander and Cherry Alexander report in their Geographical Magazine *article, "Canada's U-Turn," the outcry has been aimed at the wrong people.*

"The biggest threat to the Inuit and their culture in recent years has come from the emotional outcry over Canada's annual harp seal cull. A campaign mounted by Greenpeace and other conservation groups, illustrated with gruesome pictures of baby seals being clubbed to death on the ice, raised such a public outcry that the United States government banned all sea-mammal products from its markets. . . . Inevitably, the market for sealskins collapsed.

During the 1970s a good quality sealskin might have fetched $60 or more at a fur auction. In the spring of 1985 the average price of sealskins at one European auction was $3.68. The collapse of the sealskin market meant that northern hunting communities throughout the Arctic faced economic disaster. . . .

The Inuit were understandably bitter. They had had nothing to do with the commercial seal cull. They generally hunt adult ringed seals, the most common seal found in the Arctic. They take relatively few harp seals and they certainly don't club babies . . . to death. Understandably, the Inuit feel aggrieved that self-righteous white men did not consider the north's native people, and the important part that seal hunting plays in their existence."

A Yupik father enjoys teaching his sons hunting skills, because he feels they can benefit from his wisdom as well as from his mistakes. "I teach my boys the way I've been taught, the way my dad taught me. What I think that's wrong, I try to do it better than my dad. And when I make a mistake I try to correct it to my boys, so they'll do it better than I did."[70]

The specific skills are different now, of course. Instead of techniques of throwing harpoons, there are lessons in handling a rifle safely. But always there is the respect for nature, for the animals being hunted. And most of all, there is the constant reminder that because of the hostility of the arctic climate, Eskimo communities need to rely on one another.

"There are no Coast Guard boats nearby to rescue people if they run out of gas or get lost in the fog," says a Canadian Eskimo. "Here we are entirely on our own. We have only those in our group to rely on for survival."[71]

Even though the hunter's tools have changed, much of what he does remains the same. A seal hunter, for example, may station himself at the same breathing holes by which his ancestors squatted, patiently waiting for his prey to surface. Or he may imitate a seal, flopping across the ice, to get close to prey that is sunning itself.

Once the bullet has found its mark and the hunter has dragged the seal back to camp, the traditional roles of men and women continue to apply. Women show their daughters how to use the *ulu* knife to separate the blubber from the body of the seal. One Inupiat boy proudly describes the finesse with which his godmother tended to his first seal:

> After scraping the thick sheet of blubber from the hide, Vera cut the fat into small cubes and put them into a clean bucket. In a day or two, the oil is rendered from [melted out of] the blubber and can then be used to flavor and preserve many foods. Vera sliced the seal meat into thin strips and hung them on a wooden rack to dry.[72]

Fishing All Year Round

Fishing is another necessity for Eskimos wanting to eat country foods, and it is done all year round. Some fish are caught in nets, and others bite on a simple lure made of a shiny bottlecap or piece of aluminum foil tied to the fishing line. In Alaska, the Yupik depend on salmon and herring; the Inuit eat char and whitefish.

Eskimo dogs eat plenty of fish, too—after all, store-bought dog food is very expensive. Tiny needlefish, netted by the thousand, are scooped into dogs' bowls as a special treat. And after fish for the family have been cleaned, the bones are dried and bundled together, to be crunched up into a nutritious wintertime dog food.

For fishing expeditions, Eskimos usually set up camps. In cold weather they live in sod houses identical to the ones used by many of their parents; in warmer weather they set up tents. For many families the early summer fishing camp begins the moment children are out of school in May.

"[My husband] goes first and sets up our camp—tent, blankets, bed, clothes, pots and pans for cooking, and our grub," explains one Yupik woman who enjoys the yearly camp with her whole family. "Then we go, maybe the third week in May. We pick spring

An important part of the Eskimo diet, fish are caught year round with fishing poles and nets.

Many Eskimo families still leave their homes on the settlements for annual summer fishing expeditions. During these expeditions families camp in tents and hunt as their forebears have done for generations.

greens, go hunting, take walks. We eat fish and fresh geese. It never gets dark when we're out camping, and it's fun."[73]

Besides catching fish for their own use, many Eskimos in Alaska can make money selling them. Japanese boats wait offshore, prohibited by international law from fishing in waters too close to the United States. But no law says they cannot buy fish caught by Yupik fishermen, and they may buy as much as twenty thousand pounds of fish a year from a single Yupik entrepreneur.

A Rite of Passage

Hunting—especially seal hunting—has social effects on the community, too. For centuries proud Eskimo parents have celebrated a son's first seal with a party. Today, too, seal parties

are a much-awaited event in Eskimo communities. The celebration is not simply that of a successful hunt. The focus is on the boy himself—assuming the role of hunter, and therefore becoming a man. Although many Eskimo boys today kill their first seal by the age of eight or nine—far too young to be thought of as men—the event is still considered a rite of passage, a ceremonial introduction to adult responsibilities.

Interestingly, although men are the hunters, no men are allowed at the seal party—not even the boy who is being honored! The party is planned by the boy's mother, and preparations begin almost the moment she hears the news of the hunt.

Nowadays, the first thing the proud mother does is visit the store, where she stocks up on small food items. Cake mixes, canned fruit, tea bags, candy bars, and gum all make good favors for her party. She also may buy other items her guests might enjoy—sponges, shoelaces, batteries for a radio, candles, or matches. An especially popular favor is a can of snuff, a substance widely used by Eskimos of all ages. So common is it for children to use snuff that one visitor to the Arctic reported seeing boys and girls as young as six or seven with the telltale round imprint of the snuff can in the back pocket of their jeans.

The hostess also stocks up on widely used bulk items—flour, coffee, ten-pound bags of sugar. If the storekeeper has a particularly interesting novelty, such as eggs or fresh pineapple, she might make an impulse purchase, although it will be very expensive. Many seal parties cost a family more than $200 for the favors alone. In past years, before the advent of community grocery stores, the favors were handmade.

"There Is Nothing Restrained About It"

Women throughout the community get their invitations to the seal party over the CB radio, a device owned by almost everyone in the village. They show up happy for the mother of the hunter, and excited because of the fun they know is in store. Each guest brings a large plastic garbage bag, along with several smaller bags.

The first order of business is refreshments. The hostess dishes out hunks of seal meat and fat on plates for everyone—and guests are welcome to come back for seconds. Often bowls of *akutag* (Eskimo ice cream) are distributed, too. When the eating is over, the women pick up their large bags and gather in a tight group, for the fun, which lasts only a few minutes, is about to begin.

The hostess holds up a cloth sack, perhaps the size of a pillowcase, filled with special prizes much valued by the guests. In her novel *Eskimos: Growing Up in a Changing Culture,* Carolyn Meyer imagines a typical seal party at which the cloth sack contains

> a red fox pelt, a pair of brightly checked polyester slacks, and a few other choice items. The women crowd together, and [the hostess] throws it up over their heads, hoping that it will be caught by one person and not argued over by several. The bundle drops into the hands of one of the younger women. She is well liked, and everyone seems satisfied that she is the one to get it.[74]

After that, there are bulk items to be distributed—the coffee, the sugar, the flour. The women line up like trick-or-treaters, smiling as the hostess gives them a handful of each item, which they put into their smaller bags. As each gets her share, she quickly prepares for the final moments of the party, when the small gifts are given—or thrown—to the guests.

Eskimos use CB radios much like we use the telephone. They are owned by almost everyone.

Long arms and good jumping ability are definite advantages in this part of the seal party. The hostess stands apart from the guests and tosses the gifts high in the air. Normal Eskimo reserve is forgotten as the guests shriek and grab for the gifts. Meyer's description, though fictional, gives a good idea of the scene: "There is nothing restrained about it: the women jump, push, squeal, and grab, except for the old ladies who sit placidly out of the way."[75]

The throwing of the favors is the last part of the seal party, and as the last gift is caught, the guests leave. Often, however, they go on to another house for another party. When seal hunting is good, it is common for more than one village boy to get his first seal, and with favors at each party, the women of the community are obviously thrilled.

Villagers socialize at the annual spring festival. Eskimo celebrations are usually filled with lots of traditional food and games.

Many Excuses for a Party

Just like their forebears, modern Eskimos enjoy socializing. In Eskimo communities there are many opportunities for parties and games. "It's not only fun, it reminds us how important the community is," explains Yupik Eskimo Johnny Akuluuk. "Hunters here still share the fattest duck or the best piece of the seal with others who have none. People share the fun, too. It keeps everybody friendly, the way it should be, especially when you count on each other like we do."[76]

The blanket toss is still a favorite event at Eskimo celebrations.

Sometimes the celebrations coincide with a Canadian or American holiday such as New Year's, Thanksgiving, or even the Fourth of July, although the Eskimo festivities really have nothing to do with the calendar holidays. Many Arctic villages hold their own carnivals and festivals—some to celebrate the beginning of summer, or the end of summer, or even the midway point in the long winter. "It doesn't seem really to matter," says Akuluuk. "I think people would be glad for any excuse for a party."[77]

The celebrations are quite similar in format. There is lots of food (especially country food), and games of every sort. Eskimos still enjoy dogsled races, wrestling, and the "two-kick" game of traditional gatherings. Boys and girls play a specialized form of baseball geared for ice and snow. A softer ball is used, and it's legal to get a runner out by hitting him or her with the ball. Another contest Eskimos of all ages enjoy is the footrace. Spectators love the old women's race, where the participants prove, says novelist Meyer, "that although they may carry many years on their backs, their legs are still strong and fast."[78]

One of the most popular events at a modern Eskimo celebration is known as the *nalukatak,* or blanket toss. Thirty or more men form a circle around a large blanket—or, in more traditional celebrations, a large walrus hide with rope grips. One man gets on the blanket and the others toss him as high as possible, sometimes as high as twenty feet in the

The Exchange Dance

One of the most interesting rituals Ann Fienup-Riordan found in her life among the Yupik Eskimos in Alaska was the exchange dance. Not only does the dance provide an occasion to give thoughtful gifts to members of the community, it also allows people an opportunity to poke good-natured fun at one another. In Eskimo Essays, *Fienup-Riordan describes the dance.*

"The immediate counterpart of the seal party on Nelson Island is the men's and women's exchange dance, in which men and women are said to fight through the dance. . . . On the first night of the exchange dance, all the women in the village pair up as married couples, one woman taking the part of the husband and the other the part of the wife. Then, together, the women dance a multitude of gifts into the community hall and on the following morning give them out to the men of the village. The men perform for the women on the following evening, and the next morning the women receive gifts in their turn. The entire sequence of dances and gift-giving takes hours and hours, as everyone in the community has a turn on the dance floor.

As each mock married couple comes out to dance, they are greeted by much laughing and teasing from the audience. The particular dance that is performed is always the same, but each couple vies with the others to make its rendition particularly hilarious. Young men put mop ends on their heads for hair. Fur parkas are turned inside out to imitate age and senility, and fake muscles are pushed into the dresses of the women who are playing the role of husband."

After missionaries banned the tradition for years because they associated it with shamans, drum dancing has seen a surge in popularity in recent years.

air. The object is for the tossee to land upright on the blanket. If he is successful, he gets another turn; if not, another man is tossed.

The man being tossed is expected to throw gifts to the crowd while high in the air. In past years, pieces of baleen, tobacco, and ivory were thrown down to the laughing crowds; today, candy and gum are used instead.

Drum dancing is another activity that has gained popularity in recent years. All Eskimo dancing—especially that involving drums—was banned by missionaries throughout the Arctic. Drum dancing was a tool of the shamans, said the missionaries, and therefore anti-Christian. But this very important part of Eskimo tradition was missed, especially by the elders of the community. As one writer observes, "All during the years when there was no dancing, it remained in people's minds."[79]

It is as much fun to watch the dancers as it is to dance to the Eskimo drums. Sometimes the men drum while the women dance; other times the process is reversed.

Many of the dances are simple acting out of activities well known to the Eskimo people. "With each pulsing verse," writes Priit Vesilind, "they pantomime the traditional ways of the village: seal hunting, the thrust of the harpoon; picking salmonberries, plucking them noisily into their mouths; stalking geese."[80] And as the dancers dance, the audience enthusiastically responds to the pantomime, calling out encouragement to the dancers, and clapping.

But it is not only the traditional ways of the Eskimo that the drum dancers are acting out these days. Like other aspects of modern life in Arctic villages, this very ancient tradition sometimes compromises with the culture of the outsiders. As Vesilind noted, there was "a [part of the dance] whose movements seemed vaguely familiar—a rhythmic pulsing toward the floor with the hands, palms down, then a pushing toward the ceiling, palms up. The audience shrieked with delight. I looked with puzzlement at my guide. 'Basketball dance,' he giggled."[81]

Ice Hoops

Strangely enough, basketball is the one part of outside culture that has been universally welcomed by Alaskan Eskimos. "Venture out to the bush," says *Sports Illustrated* writer John Garrity, "to the frozen North Slope settlements of Barrow and Deadhorse, where polar bears peek in windows and the sun doesn't rise for weeks in winter . . . and you enter a realm in which basketball transcends obsession and borders on religion."[82]

A teacher at an Arctic high school agrees, and adds that the game has become as important to village life as many traditions. "Basketball is a central facet of contemporary Native culture, as much a part of life as hunting caribou, gathering spruce roots, or gill-netting salmon."[83]

High school basketball has become an energizing force for Eskimo communities. It gives teenagers something active to do in the long, boring winters. And the fierce rivalries that have been developing among high school basketball teams instill in the communities a sense of village pride. The names of the teams could not have been devised anywhere else in the world—the Tikigaq Harpoonerettes, the Aqqaluk Bears, and the Kalskag Grizzlies, to name just a few.

What makes Eskimo basketball so intriguing is the amount of travel involved. Alaskan villages are hundreds of miles apart, and many are far from roads. So instead of bus rides, Eskimo teams take planes—indeed, a team might spend $40,000 per season on travel. As one writer comments, "To anyone . . . who has played high school basketball in which a road trip is a 30-minute bus ride, a post-game burger, and a ride home the same night—the logistics and expense of bush basketball might seem outlandish."[84]

Planes, Games, and Ferry Feet

Although the Eskimo villagers themselves might be on welfare, their various tribal councils are not. Treaties and settlements with the federal government concerning oil drilling and land use have netted millions of dollars to various native tribes in Alaska. The

Two boys brave the frigid Arctic temperatures to play a game of basketball, a sport that has gained surprising popularity in Alaska.

A Language of Many Syllables

In Living Arctic, *Hugh Brody explains the structure of the Inuktitut language, and shows how many of the words are made up of long strings of other words. Also, a great deal of the vocabulary is relatively new, words created by Eskimos for things brought into their communities from the outside.*

niaquujak (resembles a head)	bread
qianattuq (causes tears)	onion
naitingujarvik (time that resembles taboo-observance)	Sunday
kiinaujak (resembles a face)	money
imuksiutik (thing for milk)	cow
kuviasukvik (happiness occasion or place)	Christmas

Newer words include:

nunakuurutik (device for going by land)	car
qangatasuuk (persistently soars)	airplane
mamaksautik (thing that makes tasty)	perfume or ketchup
uksualungniartik (one who attends to great blubber)	oil company
irqiasulaaktigijutik (device that makes you curly)	hair curler
aijuksakturlinjiik (one who fixes up one who may be in difficulty)	welfare officer or social worker

money is invested in job opportunities, industry, and the school districts. While a $40,000 travel budget for the basketball team of a small high school would be out of the question anywhere else, in the Eskimo villages in Alaska, it's a necessity.

The reliance on planes and ferryboats to shuttle a team from game to game has its drawbacks, however. Schedules are written in pencil, for the weather is never certain, and bad traveling conditions are always a threat. Most air carriers won't fly when the temperatures plummet to –30 degrees. As one pilot explains, "Mechanical things don't work well in extreme cold. And if you go down in that kind of weather, you won't survive long enough to be rescued."[85]

The hours spent in travel can be murder on a player's sense of balance. Coaches whose teams rely on ferries complain that the boats leave their players green-faced and wobbly—a condition known as "ferry feet" among basketball players. "You ride in that thing for 16 hours," says a coach, "and you just can't play ball. . . . One of our players reached down to pick up a ball, and when he straightened up, he was weaving. Believe me, you can't [even] shoot a basketball."[86]

Due to the long distances between Alaskan villages, high school basketball teams spend as much as $40,000 per season on airplane travel costs.

Facilities in Demand

But if young Eskimo athletes travel at a pace that would weary even an NBA player, the gyms in which they play their games are less than great. Some are dimly lit, others too small. One visitor to the Alaskan Arctic noted that "many of the gyms are tiny and have no room for seating; spectators line the walls, pressing so close that the rules for school games allow players to have one foot in play when they throw the ball in bounds."[87]

Amazingly, a few teams even play outside during the winter. At Kalskag High School, in southwestern Alaska, when bitter cold made the balls virtually unbounceable, players still practiced outside each day. Before their first road game, one youth told the coach he would not be able to play because he had forgotten his gloves. According to one writer, "he was reassured he wouldn't need gloves indoors."[88]

More and more gyms are being built these days, complete with glass backboards and modern scoreboards. The facilities are in great demand, too—and not just by the girls' and boys' high school teams. Throughout the community there are seniors' leagues, leagues for women, leagues for parents. The gyms often open at 5:30 each morning to accommodate all the players in the community.

How do the Eskimo players compare to players in the lower 48? Physically, Yupiks tend to be shorter than average; a tall Eskimo would certainly be far shorter than most starting players for teams in the rest of the United States. Even so, the players usually make up in strength and speed what they lack in height. And the traditional games and contests may help in their training—the coach of a winning Eskimo team claims that one of his players can kick his feet within inches of the basket!

A host of problems is tearing Eskimo villages apart. Basketball has brought a new level of competition and excitement to many young Eskimos, but the game alone has not eliminated all the rough spots. One key problem, in fact, is the inadequate education Eskimo children receive in the public schools. Since most children leave school by the eighth grade, the problem should be no surprise to anyone.

Lack of Parental Support

For many years when missionaries and governments first established schools, parents were not consulted at all. Rarely were they told what subjects their children were studying. Most parents did not understand why school was important. What they *did* understand was that their sons and daughters came back to them more confused than educated. They acted like *gussaks;* they seemed embarrassed by—or at the very least, uninterested in—the traditional ways.

More than anything, the rift in families was caused by the language problem—the children were being encouraged to speak English, but the parents and elders of the community knew only Eskimo dialects. In a culture that depended on oral tradition, the handing down of stories and ideas, this development was devastating to families. After a while, one Eskimo expert says, the elders

Schools today are attempting to get parents more involved in their children's education. A lack of parental support has made the education of young Eskimos very difficult in the past.

Many Eskimo parents fear that they have lost control of their teenagers. Blame is often placed on the white culture's values, picked up through television and rock music.

simply gave up trying. "A grandmother felt it was no longer necessary to tell the story of how an Inuit girl turned into the goddess who controls the sea," he says.[89]

But as the years have gone by, schools are trying to correct some of the earlier mistakes. Educators now realize that parental involvement is crucial to the success of Eskimo children. One school official stressed that "the only way of assuring the successful adaptation of the children is through reinforcement by adults at home. If the adults at home have been left totally in the dark as to the goals of education, they cannot perform this vital role."[90]

But many parents in Eskimo communities choose to remain separate from their children's education, and this makes teachers' jobs more difficult. "I'm tired of giving, giving, giving, and never getting anything in return," said one teacher from the Canadian Arctic. "Kids come to school dirty, their noses running, wander in at eleven o'clock. Parents don't make them come. They say education is foreign to their culture—well, so are ski-doos [snowmobiles] and video games."[91]

Other teachers agree, saying that even if a student wants to try, Eskimo houses are small and afford little privacy; thus the home may not offer the ideal environment for homework. "How can you study in a crowded house where the parents spend the night watching television?" asked one teacher.[92] And since in many villages a modern house costs $170,000, it is increasingly common for two or even three families to share a three-room house. The crowded conditions are bound to get worse—bad news for the student who needs peace and quiet to work.

In many cases, parents find that they are unable to handle their older children. They say they have less control than their own parents had, and they blame the values of the white culture, with its rock music and television. And while experts cannot state exactly what influence these cultural phenomena have actually had on Eskimo teens, they note that many Eskimo parents are reluctant to discipline their children in the first place—or if they try, they are frequently unsuccessful. Such failures affect school performance.

Rough Spots

At school children are taught with the English language only, but at home they often hear only Eskimo dialects. The result is Village English—a strange mix of both languages that makes it difficult for teachers and parents to understand their children.

"These young people need discipline to define themselves," states one sociologist. "The parents don't discipline them because they don't understand the new universe they are living in. In the past, the environment took care of the discipline."[93]

Village English

The problems with education are not limited to lack of parental involvement. Teachers attribute Eskimo children's difficulties in school largely to the language gap. Since textbooks and other materials are in English, and since few of the teachers speak any language but English, it is important that the students have a good knowledge of English, too. But that is seldom the case, especially among children who hear only Eskimo dialects spoken at home.

Teachers complain that children speak a strange mixture of English and either Yupik or Inupiat, which they have dubbed "Village English." Village English is the end product of a limited English vocabulary plugged into the language structure of an Eskimo dialect. The result, as both teachers and parents are finding out, is that students have difficulty being understood in either language.

Whereas English is a highly complex language that has almost as many exceptions as it does rules, Eskimo dialects are very regular. Moreover, they rely heavily on body language. Eyes wide open indicate that one agrees; eyes squinted shut say "no." Even from a distance, an Eskimo's actions can convey an amazing amount of information, as James Houston found when living in the Canadian Arctic:

Say I was out on Ennadai Lake, going to visit a family. The father would leap off our sled, run to the left, run back to the sled, repeat different movements on the other side, then kneel on top of the sled. He'd explain, "I'm telling my wife I've got you with me, and to bring in meat, thaw it." His wife, he knew, would have been watching us with an old brass telescope. . . . She would get the message, and put caribou meat by the lamp.[94]

Vocabulary, too, is far different in the two languages. English has lots of phrases and words that mean relatively little—for example, "How are you?" and "I am fine, thank you." To traditional Eskimos, such small talk is foolish and intrusive. If one has something to say, he or she says it without preliminary chitchat. Even "hello" and "goodbye" are not found in most Eskimo dialects.

A Rich Vocabulary

On the other hand, Eskimo languages are extraordinarily rich in specific words. For instance, linguists say that in some Eskimo dialects there are over fifty different words for "snow," for traditionally it has been important for a hunter to know whether the snow was fresh or packed down, wet or dry, and so one. Likewise, an Eskimo can with one long word give a seal's exact location on the ice.

The result of the combination of languages as different as English and Eskimo dialects is quite strange. One teacher gives "You always sometimes be go to school?" as a typical Village English sentence. Teachers say that it would be far easier to teach English to students who knew nothing of English but were fluent in their Eskimo language. "One thing we are finding out is if our children learn their first language well, they can have an easier time learning another language," says one Yupik educator. "If they are forced to learn a language [before mastering their native tongue] maybe they'll grow up illiterate in both languages."[95]

The inability of children to speak their native language has become more and more apparent to Eskimo parents. One father says that his son doesn't understand the traditional meanings of Eskimo words. "I told the boy,

iglaisillutit, untangle the dogs' leads. He stared at me," remembers the man. "He said, 'I don't have a comb with me.' He thought I was asking him to comb his hair. It's the same word. He had not learned its real meaning."[96]

The Wrong Books

But much of the blame for the problems of village education must go to the educators. It is they who determine the materials used—textbooks, workbooks, curriculum. And most of these materials are completely out of place in an Eskimo village. The reading books have no connection to things Eskimo children know about. Even if the children could read

Many of the reading books used in classrooms are inappropriate and out of place in an Eskimo village, frustrating both the teachers and students who use them.

Different Kinds of Learning

In his article "Teaching in the Fourth World," published in Phi Delta Kappan, *educator Douglas A. New explains some of the difficulties Alaskan Eskimo children have in schools.*

"The largest city most students have ever seen is Nome. Few students have seen trees, and my sons were the first children with 'lellow' (yellow) hair with whom the other students came into contact. Generally, language skills are so low and vocabulary so limited that the students have difficulty processing information that is presented to them.

Students tend to be passive learners. Traditionally, Eskimos have learned by observing. Village residents spend many hours a day, often late into the night, watching Home Box Office and wrestling. Visions of Freddy Krueger haunt the preschoolers, and from the celluloid world comes their perception of the outside world—as well as a major portion of their vocabulary. Student speakers of Village English must make the transition from concrete to abstract thinking in what is essentially their second language: the development of abstract reasoning in English is usually thus delayed."

Low language and vocabulary skills have made it difficult for many Eskimo children to succeed in school.

the stories—decode the words—how could they comprehend the meaning? As one discouraged teacher asks, "How can a student who has never seen a paved road—or, very possibly, even a car or a truck—intelligently answer a question about a traffic light?"[97]

To illustrate the frustration teachers are experiencing with such inappropriate materials, novelist Carolyn Meyer describes a teacher in a Yupik school reading aloud to the children a story of a family trout fishing in Yellowstone National Park:

He patiently explains where Yellowstone is, and how trout fishing differs from ice fishing and salmon fishing. Early in the story the family's dog encounters one of the Yellowstone bears who toys with it, tossing it into the air "like a shuttlecock."

[The teacher] draws a deep breath and describes a shuttlecock, sketching it on the chalkboard. Then he compares the game of badminton to tennis, which his students have seen on television. By the time he has finished translating the metaphor, the thread of the story is weakened and the humor of the incident is lost forever. In the next paragraph he has to start all over with a definition of "pirouette."[98]

Such frustrations are compounded on the required standardized tests, which the government uses in the allotment of school funds. Teachers worry that the questions—again, based on a lifestyle familiar to children living "outside"—will be confusing to the Eskimo children. And if they do poorly, as would be expected, how much will the school be penalized in the next budget?

What Sorts of Jobs?

Perhaps staying in school would be a more attractive option if young people felt there was something to be gained. But a good job—or just any job—is not a realistic goal in many Eskimo communities. There are sometimes temporary construction jobs, or jobs in canneries or factories hundreds of miles from home. But for the young man or woman wanting to continue to live in the home community, jobs are painfully scarce.

The white outsiders have only themselves to blame, say experts. The system seems interested in the student for too short a time, argues James Houston:

> We . . . are giving them an . . . education, then dropping them. Only a handful of Eskimos have reached university level. We're helping to jerk people out of an incredibly delicate educational system that they had devised for themselves over the centuries, and shove them into what?

Young people occasionally find work in canneries and factories away from home. But for those Eskimos who wish to stay near their home community, jobs are extremely scarce.

Does anyone propose to hire that girl as a secretary in Montreal, or have that young man run a computer in Toronto? They leave school by about the eighth grade, and meanwhile they've missed going out with their fathers and learning how to hunt, or learning from their mothers how to live off the land. All because of our monkeying around.[99]

Others agree with Houston. They say that the Eskimos who apply themselves to their studies graduate from high school and find almost no opportunities to use their knowledge of math, history, or English. Nothing has been gained by depriving them of their traditional education—parents and elders, teaching young people how to survive—and in many cases everything has been lost.

"Eskimo Adoptions"

Other disruptions occur in the lives of young people that have little to do with school. One of the most common of these is teen pregnancy. In past years, a fourteen-year-old with a young baby was common. Children matured quickly in the Arctic, and most young teenage girls were capable of making a home for children and a husband.

Now, although the village has changed, the age at which Eskimo teens have children has not. One visitor to an Arctic high school was surprised at what she saw—fourteen- and fifteen-year-old mothers. "At a Friday night dance, sultry young girls are writhing to a deafening rock song while holding babies in their arms. Babies crawl around among the dancers. 'The family is very important here,' explains the school principal."[100]

The Eskimo birthrate is now four times higher than the national average of the rest of

The Point of No Return

Although many Eskimo elders miss the old life and say they wish that they could return to more traditional times, such dreams are impossible, says Sam Hall in The Fourth World.

"There can be no return to the old life. The [outsiders'] damage is done. The Inuit cannot divorce themselves from the modern ways of the world, or from the nuclear age. Tens of thousands of Inuit . . . and other arctic dwellers are more secure now than they have ever been. Survival is no longer a central issue. The Inuit no longer face starvation. Materially, if not spiritually, there has been a vast improvement in their lives. Improved housing and health facilities, and lower infant mortality, have increased their numbers, but game stocks are no longer sufficient to support their hunting traditions. In truth, few indigenous northern dwellers would wish to face the rigors of the past. Softened by southern comfort and welfare, it is unlikely that the young are tough enough to live off the land and endure the hardships suffered by their ancestors. The hunting culture, and with it the old customs, will disappear."

the United States or Canada, and is rising each year. With the danger of starvation removed, and with improved health care, Eskimo babies are far healthier today, and that is good. However, the skyrocketing birthrate raises some worrisome questions. What will happen to all these babies being born into homes where no one is working, where houses are already overcrowded? Are Eskimo villages ready to deal with the problems that such overcrowding and poverty create?

As in the past, there is no disapproval of young teenagers having babies. No one judges their morality or behavior—it is just how things are. Besides, children are as important in the community as they were in past years—everyone loves to hold babies and play with them. Yet someone has to raise the children—and frequently it is not the mother.

One common practice from the past known as "Eskimo adoptions" still is popular. A couple with too many children to support

Teenage pregnancy has become a major problem in Eskimo communities, forcing many young girls to drop out of school.

often presented a baby to relatives or to a couple unable to have children. This way, everyone had a child to raise. And because no one worried about "owning" children, there was never a concern of keeping the identity of a child's biological parents a secret. Historians say that Eskimo children raised by adoptive parents are comfortable having two mothers and fathers.

The "adoptions" of today usually involve parents. Understanding that their teenage daughters are not really ready to be mothers, older parents take on the raising of their grandchildren. "When our two oldest girls had babies," recalls one Yupik woman, "we decided that we were going to raise them as our own, since the girls are too young. They wouldn't care for them the way we took care of them, 'cause there are so many things going on, like dances and games, and they want to be there."[101]

The raising of grandchildren is becoming common practice in Eskimo villages; nearly every family in a community has at some time adopted a child—after the death of one of their own children, or after their grown children have left home. Rarely do families complain about the arrangement, but there are problems nonetheless. Becoming pregnant disrupts the life of a teenage girl, even when she can give the child to others to raise. Many girls stop attending school after giving birth, since studying and going to classes then seem childish.

"They Are Drinking Themselves to Death"

The problem that is the most frightening to Eskimos throughout Canada and Alaska is alcoholism, and the injuries, violence, and destruction that accompany it. The entire

A drunk, passed out in front of a village bar, gets a nudge from a concerned passer-by. Alcoholism has become a monumental problem in many Eskimo communities, especially among men.

population is at risk, but teenage boys are especially vulnerable. Health officials in Eskimo villages are quick to admit that the problem is epidemic.

"They are drinking themselves to death," writes one expert on Alaska's Yupik Eskimos. "Under the influence of alcohol they are committing suicide and engaging in family violence at rates that rival the worst in the world."[102] In one village several years ago, every death was caused by alcohol. The statistics among Canadian Eskimos are frightening, too. The killers of Eskimos that rank one, two, and three are injuries, violent death, and accidents. Officials say that all three are alcohol-related.

"This is not a problem of social drinkers," says one Eskimo from Alaska. "It's not like, well, me and my buddies all drink after work and we get a little drunk. I know these guys—they drink to get drunk, and the faster the better. Not for the taste, or for the fun of being a little high. These guys drink aftershave, or vanilla extract, or even hairspray. It's ugly."[103]

Tom Kizzia, a traveler to Alaska, agrees. In his journeys he met two elders who were sick with worry about the alcohol problem in their village, Sleetmute, population 100. "They could name only two families who kept away from alcohol," he writes. "Everyone else drank to get drunk. Sometimes it seemed like everyone in the village was drinking at once."[104]

"Our Men Are In Trouble"

The violence that accompanies heavy drinking goes against everything traditional Eskimos stood for—gentleness, love of family (especially children), and a sense of community. "[The elders] told of rapes, beatings, suicides, deaths by hypothermia, all owing to alcohol," writes Kizzia. "In one family the father had been sent to prison, the mother stayed drunk, and the children had been taken by the state. Six months earlier at a party, a young man had shot his uncle to death with a rifle."[105]

Sociologists who have observed the problems in Eskimo villages agree that alcoholism reflects many frustrations, especially among men. Once the hunters whose skills kept their families from starving, Eskimo men in the late twentieth century are without purpose a great deal of the time. Even if they do

some hunting, it does not make up for being unemployed. According to a social counselor in an Alaskan Eskimo community:

Our men are in trouble. They're having a lot tougher time with this transition. They feel like they've lost their manhood. I've got a job, but my husband can't find one. He hunts a lot, fills the freezer with meat each fall. But he also watches the children, and I've become like the man of the family. And I don't like it.[106]

A priest in an Eskimo village in Canada agrees. "Women are less dependent on men now," he says. "In the time of the hunters a

Depending on Both Cultures

In his Canadian Geographic *article, "Pond Inlet: An Inuit Community Caught Between Two Worlds," David F. Pelly examines the system of Eskimo hunters in Pond Inlet for "living off the land"—a style far different from that of Eskimos just a generation ago.*

"Life for Panipakoocho [an Eskimo hunter from Pond Inlet] and the other hunters . . . is never easy. They, like their ancestors, depend on the bounty of the land and the sea. That traditional dependence persists. Our food and the food of people in the summer hunting camps we passed was caribou, char [fish], narwhal [tusked whale], and seal. Seal is the mainstay. Panipakoocho's family—his wife and five children—consumes up to three seals a week.

Unlike their ancestors, however, Panipakoocho and other residents of Pond Inlet depend equally on goods imported from the south. They live on a mixed economy. In order to buy the essentials for hunting—a boat and motor in the summer, a snowmobile in winter, plus the gas and ammunition—Panipakoocho's wife works at the Pond Inlet hotel. Occasionally, when they need extra cash, Panipakoocho works too, driving one of the trucks that regularly delivers water or pumps out waste at every house in town.

It was the same in every camp we visited: at least one of the hunters had a wife back in town who was earning money to support the hunt. It is a formula that works, but it is possible for only a limited number of Pond Inlet's families. There are simply not enough jobs to go around."

woman without a man would die. Today there is the state, and women are better educated. The men feel threatened."[107]

Many are trying to solve the problem, although it cannot be done in traditional ways. The old ways of dealing with troublemakers are no longer effective. Ridicule, having wrestling or insulting contests—even the silent treatment from the village—these approaches do not work against severe chemical abuse problems.

In recent years Eskimos have tried different methods to curb drinking. Many villages have voted to be "dry," allowing no liquor to be sold within the community. Even though the effectiveness of such legislation is limited, for there is no way the village can police each family to ensure that people are not bringing liquor in, it is a beginning.

And, say Eskimo leaders, it is good to know that most of the people in the villages want to solve the problem themselves, rather than let the white authorities from outside handle it. "We thought we'd get resistance," says an Inupiat doctor, "but people are so concerned that most communities support it. And we're going to succeed because we have our roots here and we have to live with the results."[108]

Many Eskimos agree, saying that it is difficult to expect outsiders to handle such problems—especially since many of the problems were brought to their villages by contact with the outsiders in the first place. It is not important to blame or point fingers,

No longer depended on as hunters who ensure their families' survival, many Eskimo men feel they have lost their manhood and lack purpose. These frustrations have contributed to the high rate of male alcoholism.

they say, but merely to solve the problems and regain some authority over their villages, their lives. A young Yupik man summarizes the situation:

There are some angry people in the villages—why not? They say, "remember, we had no whiskey until the whites brought it here," or "keep this in mind, that our culture has been attacked by the whites and that is the cause of problems now." But what does that solve? Never mind the past—it is the future that is waiting, and we can't step into it looking backwards.[109]

"We Must Make Our Own History"

Does it seem odd that the Eskimos of Canada and Alaska have only recently expressed a wish to solve their own problems? It shouldn't, say many Eskimos, for since the outsiders came to the Arctic, they have told the native people in many different ways that their culture was inferior and out of date in a world that was grappling with computer technology and engineering the space age. Not surprisingly, many Eskimo children have grown up feeling that they should be more like the white people who criticize them.

"I Was So Wrong"

The experience of one Inuit woman is not unusual. Inuit Ann Meekitjuk Hanson recalls:

> When I was a young girl, I wanted to be just like a [white] girl. I wore makeup. I had my cousin Sarah cut my long hair short without consent from my aunt or uncle. I was so ashamed that I wore a scarf. Eventually I had to tell them. I was very embarrassed. Then I curled my hair. I spoke English to friends even though I knew my aunt and uncle did not understand me. This made me feel that I knew more. I was so wrong.[110]

Hanson's feelings were representative of those of many Eskimo children in past years. But as time went by, more than a few came to believe that the ways of the white culture were simply too foreign, too different from their own, and not worth pursuing. One young Inuit pondered the differences between the whites and Eskimos when it came to work: "Using that little pencil. Hard going! They do so much work that doesn't look like work at all. And I thought, even if I learn things at school, I'll never be a real white man."[111]

But how is it possible to keep being Eskimos in tradition and culture without being swallowed up by the outsiders? This goal seems almost unachievable now, when jobs, health care, education, and government from the state or provincial level up are controlled by the outsiders. And how can the

Told by many outsiders that their culture is inferior and out of date, it is not surprising that many Eskimo children grow up feeling embarrassed and ashamed of their lifestyle.

The choice Eskimos face to either become modern or live in traditional ways seems to interest non-Eskimos as well. As Hugh Brody points out in Living Arctic, *white society is often impatient and irritated with people who cannot make up their minds which world they want to live in.*

"How can people use dog teams as well as snowmobiles? How can they live in both snow houses and prefabricated bungalows? How can they depend upon both the harpoon and the rifle? . . . How can they exist, at one and the same time, in the past and the present? It is all too easy for us to express incredulity, and even indignation, over these seeming inconsistencies. . . .

And so we force a moral choice on [Eskimos] . . . traditional or modern. They must be one or the other. We challenge and reproach them with the question. . . . Hunters who rely on rifles are sneered at by romantic purists who believe that only a hunter with a harpoon or bow and arrows is really a hunter. Hunters who insist on using worn and battered .30/.30's are despised for failure to understand the advantages of the telescopic sight.

Men and women wearing wool trousers and down parkas are scorned for 'failing' to rely on caribou and moose-hide clothing. People who do wear skin clothing are looked down on as backward or romanticized as representatives of the stone age. . . . Inuit who encouraged their children to spend time on the land rather than in school are warned that they are jeopardizing the next generation's best prospects. Inuit who collect welfare payments are felt to have let down both us and themselves."

Eskimos correct wrongs that have been done to them, which continue to affect the way they live? Alaskan and Canadian Eskimos have been wrestling with these questions in recent years, especially as problems in their villages become more and more apparent.

"We Never Go and Bark"

But to solve their problems, the Eskimos need more control, more self-determination. They have given up so much, they say, that outsiders have taken all the power. Lacking a voice in matters that affect them, the Eskimos have endured massive abuse of their traditions. The time has come, say Eskimo leaders, to set limits on native hospitality.

"When newcomers ignore requests that hunters' and trappers' rights be respected and their system of law be followed, patience becomes inappropriate," argues expert Hugh Brody. "When culture and material loss put survival itself at stake, gentleness achieves very little."[112]

One Inuit feels that the Eskimos haven't been loud enough, that they have allowed themselves to be constrained by the whites:

The other day I was taking a walk, and I passed a house there with a dog tied outside. I didn't notice it and all of a sudden this dog jumped up and gave me a big bark, and then after I passed through there, I was saying to myself, "Well, that dog taught me a lesson."

You know, so often you see the native people, they are tied down too much, I think, by the government. We never go and bark, therefore nobody takes notice of us and it is about time that we the people of this northland should get up sometime and bark.[113]

New Weapons

The way Eskimos have been "barking" lately is far different from any kind of problem solving they have done. To settle disputes with the outsiders, they have had to begin using new tools—politics and law—both foreign to the tradition of Eskimo communities. By becoming involved in the use of their land and the direction of their communities, Eskimos have achieved interesting results.

The first foray into politics came after 1968, when oil was discovered in Alaska. Oil companies swarmed into the north country, eager to be the first to sink their wells. They also planned a huge pipeline that would carry the oil across the state to tankers, which in turn would transport it to refineries. The Eskimos knew the pipeline would dramatically affect the land, the animals, and their communities.

This time they spoke out against the outsiders. They pointed out that the U.S. government had neglected to settle old native claims to the land. How, they asked, could the United States pretend to "own" land that had been inhabited by Eskimos and other native people for thousands of years? One Eskimo leader went before Congress, saying, "If the United States government is prepared to buy the Arctic Slope or rent it, the Eskimos are prepared to discuss terms."[114]

The result of the negotiations was the Alaska Native Land Claim Settlement Act (ANLCSA). In this piece of legislation, the

Eskimos attend a community council meeting. In recent years Eskimos have become more involved in the decision-making process in their communities.

A tanker creates an artificial island for an Arctic oil drilling rig. Oil companies flocked to the Far North after the 1968 discovery of oil in Alaska.

government took over 330 million acres of land and compensated the Eskimos by granting them a cash settlement of $962.5 million, as well as a land settlement, 44 million acres, which is more than 10 percent of the state's acreage. ANLCSA replaced the system used in the lower 48 states—that of the government creating reservations for native people. It was the beginning of a new kind of life for Eskimo communities.

Mixed Blessing

Some might have viewed ANLCSA as a great victory for the Yupiks and other Alaskan natives, but Eskimo leaders felt it was a compromise. It would have been far better if Eskimos had not had to give up any land at all, said leader Joe Upicksoun. "We . . . Eskimos have never wanted money as such—we wanted land, because out of the land we would make our money. We would protect our subsistence living; we would still have our heritage."[115]

The money from ANLCSA was not paid to individuals; rather, money was invested in village "corporations." Villages and regions could invest the money in businesses and industries that could help create jobs and bolster the economy. According to the legislation, after twenty years had passed, not only could regional corporations develop the land and its resources, they could transfer ownership, if they so chose.

ANLCSA has been a disappointment to many Eskimos. Much of the cash settlement went toward putting the legislation into effect. What perhaps seemed like a great deal of money did not stretch very far, especially with people who were unaccustomed to developing and administering wide-ranging programs. One University of Alaska economics professor feels the Eskimos were too new to the legislative and political process to handle ANLCSA wisely: "Suppose you uprooted a bunch of successful Fortune 500 businessmen, gave them some whale boats, rifles, and snowmachines, and said, 'Okay, you have 20 years to make a go of subsistence.' That's the enormity of the gap."[116]

By 1990 most village and regional corporations were floundering. As the *Alaska Business Monthly* reported, "By all accounts, this experiment has been heartbreaking and almost incalculably costly, in both financial and human terms."[117] Legal fees and administrative costs have been enormous, and the Eskimos, to whom the idea of "ownership" is culturally alien, are fighting among themselves to determine the correct path to follow. Is the goal a thriving cash economy? To lure businesses and industry to the North by selling off their land? Or perhaps to be left alone, to permit a return to a traditional Eskimo lifestyle?

Human Animals in a Cultural Zoo

And so, as more and more outsiders have come to the North, Eskimos have become increasingly involved in their doings. Hunters, fishermen, and tourists wanting to capture polar bears and walrus on film—all have been lured to the Arctic to see what cannot be seen anywhere else on earth. Canada spends more than a million dollars yearly enticing Americans and Europeans to visit the "untouched primitive wilderness of the Arctic." Alaska, too, encourages sportsmen to hunt and fish there.

But some experts have worried that Eskimos will be losers in such a business. "The danger," writes historian Sam Hall, "is that the people of the north will become human animals in a cultural zoo, mere objects of curiosity for adventurous southerners, wealthy enough to enjoy the temptations of glossy travel magazines, luxury cruises through the icebergs, reindeer roundups, or photographic safaris among walrus and polar bears."[118]

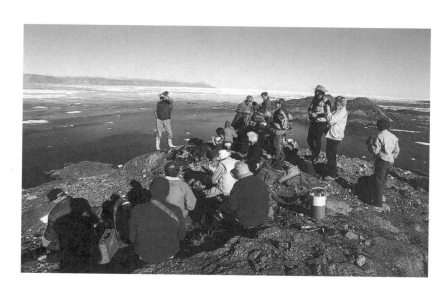

Tourism has become big business in the Arctic. Hunters, fishermen, and tourists alike are lured to the beautiful wilderness.

In fact, many Eskimos have already experienced the feeling of being "objects of curiosity," and they find it distasteful. "Everybody who comes to [the village] wants only to look at the people and say, 'Look at the stupid-looking people,'" says one Canadian Inuit. "We all thought we'd leave the land and make money off the tourists. Now we're waking up."[119]

The money is good, however, and some Eskimos welcome tourism even though they dislike the attitude of some of the tourists. Being a hunting guide is especially profitable, say some Eskimos. On Nunivak Island off the west coast of Alaska, sportsmen pay guides from $5,000 to $7,000, a fee that also covers food, a bed for a night in an Eskimo home (there are no lodges or hotels on the island), and the use of a snowmobile.

In addition to paying top dollar for the chance to shoot a musk ox or other arctic animal, the outsiders often leave their guides big tips—a custom that astonishes the Eskimos. "Sometimes they're so happy with the trophy [game hunted] that they tip you $200, $400. Those businessmen!" said one Eskimo guide wonderingly.[120]

Compromising Tradition?

But many Eskimos resent the presence of the outsiders. They feel that by encouraging whites to visit their communities, Eskimo people are compromising their traditions. Some Eskimo leaders are especially worried because the balance of nature is being upset.

Tourists watch an Eskimo skin a seal. Although Arctic tourism is profitable for many natives, some Eskimos resent the outsiders and complain of feeling like "objects of curiosity."

The Death of a River

In The Wake of the Unseen Object: Among the Native Cultures of Bush Alaska, *Tom Kizzia describes the anger and outrage felt by Eskimo village leaders when they discovered that the Tuluksak, a river on which they depended, was being poisoned by miners.*

"The people of Tuluksak travel on the river, fish in it, and pump it for drinking water, so they were quite naturally alarmed when the water turned cloudy in June a few years earlier. The river was so muddy the elders said it was going to flood, but it didn't rise. People got diarrhea and quit drinking from the river. The water turned rusty and orange, and it left a funny stain, so that all summer riverboats from Tuluksak could be recognized along the Kuskokwim [the channel into which the Tuluksak flows] by a brown waterline, like the line in a toilet bowl.

Finally the village leaders chartered a plane and flew to the mountains, where they discovered bulldozers tearing up the riverbed to get at gold. To stop them, the village sought help from Calista, the regional Native corporation, but Calista had its own mineral deposits [in nearby mountains] and chose to remain on the sidelines. Anna, who was mayor at the time, led Tuluksak to court. The miners, it turned out, had a legal claim to the river under federal mining laws written in 1872."

One clear example is found in the treatment of animals. Visitors to the Arctic report Inuit pilots flying dangerously low over polar bears and seals, buzzing yards over the frightened animals' heads so that their passengers can get a good look at the wildlife. In some areas, Eskimo guides take visitors over the ice in large, enclosed sleds pulled by snowmobiles, so that their customers can hunt seals in relative warmth and comfort. Observers say that while the hunters are pampered in enclosed sleds, the seals suffer. The marksmanship of many of these hunters is poor, and they fail to kill their prey quickly. Rather, they wound the seals, which eventually slither below the ice to die.

Sometimes Eskimo traditions are violated unknowingly by outsiders. In parts of Alaska, for example, Yupik guides watch in disgust as visiting sportsmen fish for fun— a concept foreign to Eskimo people. "Many of the sportsmen considered themselves good conservationists," explains one writer, "because they practiced hook-and-release fishing. Some even used barbless hooks. These fishermen, who sometimes felt the local hostility, would undoubtedly be confused [to learn] that hook-and-release fishing was offensive to Yupik tradition, which held that it was disrespectful to play with animals and catch what you didn't want to eat."[121]

Blowouts and Black Ice

Tourism and sportsmen are not alone in exerting negative effects on the delicately balanced environment of the Arctic. The increased presence of industries—especially mining and oil—has many Eskimo leaders

Many Eskimo leaders fear that the increased presence of oil tankers in the Arctic makes oil spills likely. A large oil spill would be devastating to the wildlife populations that some Eskimos still depend on.

worried. Oil spills and heavy air and sea traffic have already passed through the Arctic waters, and still the corporations and industries continue to expand.

In Canada, the petroleum and mining industries have been demanding that the sea lanes in the northwest be kept clear of ice for longer periods of the year. (As it is, there is a window of only two or three months when the ice thaws enough for ships to get through to oil and ore sites.) After all, say the industries, the technology is there—special ships called icebreakers can crunch through the ice to make paths for the ships.

But Eskimos don't like the idea. The waters in the northwest are loaded with deadly icebergs that can rip even the sturdiest ship to shreds. No icebreaker can make a dent in an iceberg. What will happen when loaded tankers are gutted by the ice, and oil pours into the water? What will become of the walrus, the fish, the thousands of birds that make their home in or near those waters?

Eskimo leaders in Alaska and Canada feel that the outside industries are indifferent to the ecology of their land. "The oil people do not care about fish, the seals, and the birds," states the Eskimo mayor of one Alaskan village. "They will come for oil to make money so they can eat their kinds of food. They eat through money."[122]

Another elder in the community agrees. "The land, the water, and the air are never the same again. . . . Oilmen make noise and spill things into the water. Even when they try to be careful, they are going to change things."[123]

One very large worry, especially in Canada, is the possibility of an oil blowout—the uncontrolled outpouring of oil from a newly drilled well. A blowout anywhere is a catastrophe—it means oil gushing into the sea or the surrounding countryside. But in the Arctic it would be far more devastating. Engineers would have to let the oil keep gushing until May, when the ice melts enough to permit specialized crews to cap the blowout. Even a moderate blowout, say experts, would spill half a million barrels of oil into the sea.

Contaminated water would not be the only result. Sheets of ice would carry the oil with them as they slowly move about, creating what is called "black ice." Fish, seals, birds—all wildlife even a thousand miles away—would be poisoned by the oil and black ice. The entire food chain upon which some Eskimos still rely would be wiped out.

Back to the Land

Fed up with the intrusion of outsiders and the problems they create, some Eskimos are choosing a different route. In Canada, for instance, Eskimos are giving up their homes in the settlements established by the government and moving back to the traditional hunting camps. Interestingly, the government is helping, by means of the Outpost Camp Program, which makes available financial help to people who want to return to the land. Each hunting camp is given a grant, which permits Eskimos to buy materials to build small wooden and sod huts. There is also gas money for outboard motors and snowmobiles, and an allotment of four gallons of heating fuel per day between September and May. Participants can borrow a two-way radio, as well as a medical kit. Some camps even allow low-interest loans for

Coming Back to the Villages

Although many young Eskimos talk about getting out of their villages someday and traveling to the places they see on television, some Eskimos leave their villages only to return again. In his article "Hunters of the Lost Spirit," for National Geographic, *writer Priit Vesilind records a conversation with a Yupik Eskimo woman who had lived in the lower 48 for thirteen years before returning to Alaska.*

"'Regardless of where I was or what I did,' she said, 'I knew that I belonged to some place back here. There's a lot of security and a sense of peace and fullness that comes from that—knowing that I belong here and that these people belong to me. They understand. And I'm part of the land. I know it's different with the regular Anglo. But I didn't even wear diapers when I was a kid. I was in a sod house till I was 11 years old.

'Last summer we went berry picking and camping near old Chevak [near the west coast of Alaska, north of Nunivak Island]. It's a powerful experience just to know that your ancestors lived in that area for thousands of years. Even though I'm supposed to be educated, even though I know the scientific method, I still feel their spirits.'"

Some Eskimos are choosing to return to a simpler life found in traditional hunting camps. Through the Outpost Camp Program, the Canadian government makes financial assistance available to those Eskimos who wish to live closer to the land.

the purchase of ammunition, tools, or other essentials.

The program is certainly not for everyone. As Bryan and Cherry Alexander report, "Some young Inuits didn't take to the traditional camp life, and, after their initial enthusiasm waned, reverted to the rock music, videos, and coffee bars of the modern Arctic settlements."[124] But many did stay, and have found a far more peaceful life—though not as easy—battling nature rather than butting heads with the outsiders.

Whether Eskimos in the outposts will be able to remain separate for a long time is uncertain, for as oil and minerals are increasingly sought after, even the remote hunting camp communities will perhaps be invaded. But for the time being, say these camp dwellers, they are much happier where they are.

The Future of the Real People

It is not certain how, or even whether, the Eskimos of Alaska and Canada will solve their problems. Some worry that the culture and traditions of the Eskimos will be, for all purposes, dead within a generation. They point to most young people's lack of interest in the old ways, and to the erosion of traditional Eskimo communities.

One Eskimo speaks sadly of the loss of the sense of sharing, the glue that bound people together in past generations. "Now, in the communities, that cooperation is gone," says elder Simon Akpaliapik. "In some places hunters are selling their meat, even to relatives."[125] Although this does not happen in every community, the practice seems to be more common every month, as times get tighter, say some Eskimos.

Two Different Ways

It seems that the Eskimo people are being tugged in two different directions. On one side, they are being told to modernize and join the shrinking global economy—complete with all the problems that leap entails. Many Eskimos think this is the way, saying that although the back-to-the-land programs might sound tempting, the future of the

Under constant pressure to modernize, the Eskimos are finding it increasingly difficult to keep their culture and traditions alive.

Looking Ahead

Alice and Billy Rivers are Yupik Eskimos living in Scammon Bay, Alaska. In this excerpt from In Two Worlds: A Yupik Eskimo Family, *by Aylette Jenness and Alice Rivers, the couple talk about the differences between their lives and their children's.*

"Alice says, 'When I was a kid, I used to do things with my mom. I used to watch her sew. Now I try to have Mattie knit, crochet, make things, but she thinks it's too boring. She knows how to do it, but she can't sit and look at one thing for a long time. I can't even teach her how to sew a skin. She doesn't have any patience.

'Now there's so many other things going on. In our time there was no basketball, no Igloo [video arcade], hardly any dances.'

Billy says, 'When I was Billy Junior's age, I used to run maybe twenty or thirty times around a pond with my little wooden boat. Just run around, play with it, put mud inside of it, and run around. I'd never think of TV, it wasn't in my mind.

'Everything is not the same here in Alaska, not like before. Things are changing. Things are getting more expensive. Most of the people are depending on more jobs. I mean working, you have to have a job. I talk to the kids, I just say what we'd like them to do. I tell them, "If you go to school, and be smart over there, and try to learn what you're taught, you guys will have good jobs, and good-paying jobs. I want you to have good-paying jobs, so we'll have the things that we need, anything we need"; like this I talk to them.'"

Eskimos cannot be achieved by the traditional route. "You can't go back," says a priest in an Eskimo village. "The way to the future is through education and integration into the modern world." [126]

On the other hand, however, the wisest of the elders often tug in the other direction. Leah Nuturaq was born 104 years ago in the Canadian Arctic. She knows no English and has never been interested in learning. When writer George Tombs visited her, she was curled up in bed, with a bowl of fresh seal brains on the nightstand beside her. Her advice to her people was as traditional as her choice of snack.

"I tell the young people what my elders used to tell me," she says in her Eskimo dialect. "Listen to the Inuit way of life and not the white man's way. . . . I listened. I never said no to my elders, I respected them. And I feel that is the reason I have been given a longer life." [127]

"The Only Hope"

But there is a third direction, and some Eskimos have chosen it. Although it is difficult, it is perhaps the only one that gives realistic hope to the Real People. It is the direction of some of the Yupik students Doug Meeker taught at an Alaskan high school. Meeker says that these were not necessarily the brightest and the most motivated of his students, but he observes:

These are the kids that I see being the only hope of the Eskimo people. They are the ones who learned their language—probably from their grandparents. And they understand the tradition, the culture. They aren't ashamed of being Eskimos, either.

The only hope for the Eskimo people may lie with those children who express pride in their heritage, and who are making an effort to learn the language, culture, and traditions of their ancestors.

On the other hand, these kids were able to understand the system that the white culture placed on them, too. At a very gut level they were able to be part of Western culture—how could they help it? And also they were very much Yupik. They valued the system of their ancestors.[128]

Some of Meeker's students did go on to college—maybe the University of Alaska, or even schools in the lower 48. "But they weren't interested in being Eskimos any more," he says. "They got out, and they were through. The kids I have hope for are the ones who return to their villages and give back to their people. These are the future, I think."[129]

Whatever path the Eskimos choose—economically, politically, socially—one thing is very certain. Unlike their parents and grandparents, the Eskimos today, because of where they live, are becoming an integral part of a much larger world. The decisions made in the town meetings and tribal councils of remote Eskimo villages may well determine the future of the Real People.

Notes

Introduction: "Two Inches Above the Television Screen"

1. Interview, January 1994, Johnny Akuluuk.
2. Carole Beaulieu, "Between Hunting and Hard Rock," *World Press Review,* July 1992.

Chapter 1: Traditions of the Real People

3. Aylette Jenness and Alice Rivers, *In Two Worlds: A Yupik Eskimo Family.* Boston: Houghton Mifflin, 1989.
4. Mary D. Kierstead, "The Man: A Profile of James Houston," *The New Yorker,* August 29, 1988.
5. Hugh Brody, *Living Arctic: Hunters of the Canadian North.* Seattle: University of Washington Press, 1987.
6. Jenness and Rivers, *In Two Worlds.*
7. Ernest Burch Jr., *The Eskimos.* Norman: University of Oklahoma Press, 1988.
8. Waldo Bodfish Sr., *Kusiq: An Eskimo Life History from the Arctic Coast of Alaska.* Fairbanks: University of Alaska Press, 1991.
9. Carolyn Meyer, *Eskimos: Growing Up in a Changing Culture.* New York: Atheneum, 1977.
10. Sam Hall, *The Fourth World: The Heritage of the Arctic and Its Destruction.* New York: Knopf, 1987.
11. Hall, *The Fourth World.*
12. Brody, *Living Arctic.*
13. Hall, *The Fourth World.*
14. Hall, *The Fourth World.*
15. Hall, *The Fourth World.*

Chapter 2: For the Good of the Community

16. Louis Alianakuluk, quoted in Brody, *Living Arctic.*
17. Hall, *The Fourth World.*
18. James Houston, quoted in Kierstead, "The Man."
19. Quoted in Brody, *Living Arctic.*
20. Quoted in Kierstead, "The Man."
21. Hall, *The Fourth World.*
22. Hall, *The Fourth World.*
23. Hall, *The Fourth World.*
24. Quoted in Kierstead, "The Man."
25. Paul M. Elliott, *Eskimos of the World.* New York: Julian Messner, 1976.
26. Norman A. Chance, *The Eskimos of North Alaska.* New York: Holt, Rinehart, and Winston, 1966.
27. Brody, *Living Arctic.*
28. Interview, Johnny Akuluuk.
29. Burch, *The Eskimos.*
30. Quoted in Burch, *The Eskimos.*

Chapter 3: The Coming of the Outsiders

31. Richard Hakluyt, quoted in Ann Fienup-Riordan, *Eskimo Essays.* New Brunswick, NJ: Rutgers University Press, 1990.
32. Hall, *The Fourth World.*
33. Hall, *The Fourth World.*
34. Hall, *The Fourth World.*
35. Richard Adams Carey, *Raven's Children: An Alaskan Culture at Twilight.* Boston: Houghton Mifflin, 1992.
36. Carey, *Raven's Children.*
37. Quoted in Tom Kizzia, *The Wake of the Unseen Object: Among the Native Cultures of Bush Alaska.* New York: Henry Holt, 1991.

38. Hall, *The Fourth World.*
39. Quoted in Elliott, *Eskimos of the World.*

Chapter 4: "In Their Best Interests"

40. Quoted in Bodfish, *Kusiq.*
41. Bodfish, *Kusiq.*
42. Wendell H. Oswalt, *Bashful No Longer: An Alaskan Eskimo Ethnohistory, 1778–1988.* Norman: University of Oklahoma Press, 1990.
43. Oswalt, *Bashful No Longer.*
44. Hall, *The Fourth World.*
45. Hall, *The Fourth World.*
46. Hall, *The Fourth World.*
47. Hall, *The Fourth World.*
48. Hall, *The Fourth World.*
49. Quoted in Jurgen E. Boden and Elke Boden, eds., *Canada North of Sixty.* Toronto: McClelland and Stewart, 1991.
50. Simon Anaviapik, quoted in Brody, *Living Arctic.*
51. R. Quinn Duffy, *The Road to Nunavut: The Progress of the Eastern Arctic Inuit Since the Second World War.* Kingston, Quebec: McGill–Queens University Press, 1988.
52. Paula Younkin, *Indians of the Arctic and Subarctic.* New York: Facts on File, 1992.
53. Younkin, *Indians of the Arctic and Subarctic.*
54. Duffy, *The Road to Nunavut.*
55. Meyer, *Eskimos: Growing Up in a Changing Culture.*
56. Interview, Johnny Akuluuk.
57. Quoted in Kizzia, *The Wake of the Unseen Object.*
58. Quoted in Duffy, *The Road to Nunavut.*
59. Hall, *The Fourth World.*
60. Interviews, November 1993–January 1994, Doug Meeker.
61. George Tombs, "Canada's New Arctic," *World Monitor,* July 1990.

62. Interview, Johnny Akuluuk.
63. Hall, *The Fourth World.*
64. Bryan Alexander and Cherry Alexander, "Canada's U-Turn," *The Geographical Magazine,* November 1988.

Chapter 5: Day to Day: Life in the Community

65. Hall, *The Fourth World.*
66. Quoted in Duffy, *The Road to Nunavut.*
67. Meyer, *Eskimos: Growing Up in a Changing Culture.*
68. Jenness and Rivers, *In Two Worlds.*
69. Quoted in Diane Hoyt-Goldsmith, *Arctic Hunter.* New York: Holiday House, 1992.
70. Quoted in Jenness and Rivers, *In Two Worlds.*
71. Quoted in Hoyt-Goldsmith, *Arctic Hunter.*
72. Quoted in Hoyt-Goldsmith, *Arctic Hunter.*
73. Quoted in Jenness and Rivers, *In Two Worlds.*
74. Meyer, *Eskimos: Growing Up in a Changing Culture.*
75. Meyer, *Eskimos: Growing Up in a Changing Culture.*
76. Interview, Johnny Akuluuk.
77. Interview, Johnny Akuluuk.
78. Meyer, *Eskimos: Growing Up in a Changing Culture.*
79. Jenness and Rivers, *In Two Worlds.*
80. Priit Vesilind, "Hunters of the Lost Spirit," *National Geographic,* February 1983.
81. Vesilind, "Hunters of the Lost Spirit."
82. John Garrity, "Ice Buckets," *Sports Illustrated,* January 31, 1994.
83. Quoted in Garrity, "Ice Buckets."
84. Garrity, "Ice Buckets."
85. Quoted in Garrity, "Ice Buckets."
86. Quoted in Garrity, "Ice Buckets."
87. Kizzia, *The Wake of the Unseen Object.*
88. Kizzia, *The Wake of the Unseen Object.*

Chapter 6: Rough Spots

89. Quoted in Kierstead, "The Man."
90. Quoted in Duffy, *The Road to Nunavut.*
91. Quoted in Vesilind, "Hunters of the Lost Spirit."
92. Quoted in Beaulieu, "Between Hunting and Hard Rock."
93. Quoted in Beaulieu, "Between Hunting and Hard Rock."
94. Quoted in Kierstead, "The Man."
95. Quoted in Kizzia, *The Wake of the Unseen Object.*
96. Quoted in Brody, *Living Arctic.*
97. Quoted in Douglas A. New, "Teaching in the Fourth World," *Phi Delta Kappan,* January 1992.
98. Meyer, *Eskimos: Growing Up in a Changing Culture.*
99. Quoted in Kierstead, "The Man."
100. Quoted in Beaulieu, "Between Hunting and Hard Rock."
101. Quoted in Jenness and Rivers, *In Two Worlds.*
102. Fienup-Riordan, *Eskimo Essays.*
103. Interview, Johnny Akuluuk.
104. Kizzia, *The Wake of the Unseen Object.*
105. Kizzia, *The Wake of the Unseen Object.*
106. Quoted in Vesilind, "Hunters of the Lost Spirit."
107. Quoted in Beaulieu, "Between Hunting and Hard Rock."
108. Quoted in Vesilind, "Hunters of the Lost Spirit."
109. Interview, Johnny Akuluuk.

Chapter 7: "We Must Make Our Own History"

110. Quoted in Boden, *Canada North of Sixty.*
111. Quoted in Brody, *Living Arctic.*
112. Brody, *Living Arctic.*
113. Jim Sittichinli, quoted in Brody, *Living Arctic.*
114. Quoted in Younkin, *Indians of the Arctic and Subarctic.*
115. Quoted in Lisa Drew, "Here's Your Land, Now Make Money," *National Wildlife,* December 1992/January 1993.
116. Quoted in Drew, "Here's Your Land, Now Make Money."
117. Quoted in Drew, "Here's Your Land, Now Make Money."
118. Hall, *The Fourth World.*
119. Quoted in Vesilind, "Hunters of the Lost Spirit."
120. Brad Reynolds and Don Doll, "Eskimo Hunters of the Bering Sea," *National Geographic,* June 1984.
121. Kizzia, *The Wake of the Unseen Object.*
122. Quoted in Reynolds and Doll, "Eskimo Hunters of the Bering Sea."
123. Quoted in Reynolds and Doll, "Eskimo Hunters of the Bering Sea."
124. Alexander and Alexander, "Canada's U-Turn."

Conclusion: The Future of the Real People

125. Quoted in David F. Pelly, "Pond Inlet: An Inuit Community Caught Between Two Worlds," *Canadian Geographic,* February/March 1991.
126. Quoted in Beaulieu, "Between Hunting and Hard Rock."
127. Quoted in Tombs, "Canada's New Arctic."
128. Interview, Doug Meeker.
129. Interview, Doug Meeker.

For Further Reading

Frederick Bruemmer, *Seasons of the Eskimos: A Vanishing Way of Life.* Greenwich, CT: New York Graphic Society, 1971. Good material on traditional Eskimo life; excellent photographs.

Ernest Burch Jr., *The Eskimos.* Norman: University of Oklahoma Press, 1988. Excellent photographs; good description of hunting and fishing customs of Eskimos.

Lisa Drew, "Here's Your Land, Now Make Money," *National Wildlife,* December 1992/January 1993. Good discussion of the problems of land development in Eskimo territories.

Paul M. Elliott, *Eskimos of the World.* New York: Julian Messner, 1976. Somewhat dated, but very good, readable account of the history of Eskimos.

Arlene Hirschfelder, *Happily May I Walk.* New York: Scribner's, 1986. Easy-to-read background chapter on native peoples of Alaska.

Diane Hoyt-Goldsmith, *Arctic Hunter.* New York: Holiday House, 1992. Easy reading. Good, up-to-date profile of young Inupiat boy's life in Alaska.

Carolyn Meyer, *Eskimos: Growing Up in a Changing Culture.* New York: Atheneum, 1977. Though fictional, the book gives a good picture of the conflicts experienced by Eskimo villages today.

Johnny Akuluuk, personal interview, January 1994.

Bryan Alexander and Cherry Alexander, "Canada's U-Turn," *The Geographical Magazine*, November 1988. Fascinating story of Eskimos who are trying to regain their past culture.

Carole Beaulieu, "Between Hunting and Hard Rock," *World Press Review*, July 1992. Excellent article showing crises facing Eskimo teens in Canada's Arctic.

Jurgen F. Boden and Elke Boden, eds., *Canada North of Sixty*. Toronto: McClelland and Stewart, 1991. Most of the book deals with the flora and fauna of the north of Canada, but the excellent photographs can help the reader gain a feeling for the Eskimos' environment.

Waldo Bodfish Sr., *Kusiq: An Eskimo Life History from the Arctic Coast of Alaska.* Fairbanks: University of Alaska Press, 1991. Extremely helpful endnotes and index.

Jean L. Briggs, *Never in Anger: Portrait of an Eskimo Family.* Cambridge, MA: Harvard University Press, 1970. Detailed account of every aspect of rearing children among native people in the Canadian Northwest Territories.

Hugh Brody, *Living Arctic: Hunters of the Canadian North.* Seattle: University of Washington Press, 1987. Superb photographs and interesting text describing the Eskimos' survival in the cold of the Arctic.

Richard Adams Carey, *Raven's Children: An Alaskan Culture at Twilight.* Boston: Houghton Mifflin, 1992. Interesting narrative of travels among Alaska's Yupik Eskimos.

Norman A. Chance, *The Eskimo of North Alaska.* New York: Holt, Rinehart, and Winston, 1966. Excellent bibliography; good chapter on the kinds of change anticipated by Eskimos.

Robert Coles and Jane Hallowell Coles, *Women of Crisis: Lives of Struggle and Hope.* New York: Delacorte Press, 1978. Interesting interview with an Eskimo woman of Alaska; fascinating discussion of the spiritual side of Eskimo life in modern times.

Richard G. Condon, *Inuit Behavior and Seasonal Change in the Canadian Arctic.* Ann Arbor, MI: UMI Research Press, 1981. Difficult reading, but excellent bibliography and reference notes.

R. Quinn Duffy, *The Road to Nunavut: The Progress of the Eastern Arctic Inuit Since the Second World War.* Kingston, Quebec: McGill–Queens University Press, 1988. Helpful in understanding postwar politics of Eskimos in Canada.

Ann Fienup-Riordan, *Eskimo Essays.* New Brunswick, NJ: Rutgers University Press, 1990. Very helpful in recognizing white stereotypes of Yupik Eskimos. Excellent bibliography.

William W. Fitzhugh and Susan A. Kaplan, eds., *Inua: Spirit World of the Bering Sea Eskimo.* Helpful photographs and historical quotations.

John Garrity, "Ice Buckets," *Sports Illustrated*, January 31, 1994. A sportswriter's view of the impact of basketball on the Arctic. Excellent photographs.

Sam Hall, *The Fourth World: The Heritage of the Arctic and Its Destruction.* New York: Knopf, 1987. Very thorough yet readable account of the history of the Eskimos' relationship with white culture.

Aylette Jenness and Alice Rivers, *In Two Worlds: A Yupik Eskimo Family.* Boston: Houghton Mifflin, 1989. Invaluable for both its black-and-white photographs and readable text. Helpful bibliography.

Joseph G. Jorgensen, *Oil Age Eskimos.* Berkeley: University of California Press, 1990. A scholarly study of three Eskimo villages and their use of natural resources.

Mary D. Kierstead, "The Man: A Profile of James Houston," *The New Yorker,* August 29, 1988. Very readable biographical essay about a man who lived much of his life among Eskimos.

Tom Kizzia, *The Wake of the Unseen Object: Among the Native Cultures of Bush Alaska.* New York: Henry Holt, 1991. Very exciting account of travels in northern Alaska; especially helpful section on Eskimo history.

Douglas Meeker, personal interviews; November 1993–January 1994.

Douglas A. New, "Teaching in the Fourth World," *Phi Delta Kappan,* January 1992. Helpful article, showing the difficulties encountered by students and teachers in Eskimo schools.

Wendell H. Oswalt, *Bashful No Longer: An Alaskan Eskimo Ethnohistory, 1778–1988.* Norman: University of Oklahoma Press, 1990. Excellent index and bibliography.

David F. Pelly, "Pond Inlet: An Inuit Community Caught Between Two Worlds," *Canadian Geographic,* February/March 1991. Interesting insights about some of the difficulties facing many Canadian Eskimos.

Brad Reynolds and Don Doll, "Eskimo Hunters of the Bering Sea," *National Geographic,* June 1984. Very readable; excellent photographs.

Julie E. Sprott, *Alaska Native Parents in Anchorage: Perspectives on Childrearing.* Lanham, MD: University Press of America, 1992. Helpful interviews with parents about the challenges of raising Eskimo children in a white culture.

Through Yupik Eyes (poetry and photographs by students of St. Mary's High School). Anchorage, AK: Van Cleve Press, 1976. Invaluable background to material to promote an appreciation of Yupik culture.

George Tombs, "Canada's New Arctic," *World Monitor,* July 1990. Helpful summary of Eskimos' economic and educational problems.

Priit Vesilind, "Hunters of the Lost Spirit," *National Geographic,* February 1983. Excellent photographs and text illustrating the strong public demand for self-government.

Paula Younkin, *Indians of the Arctic and Subarctic.* New York: Facts on File, 1992. Helpful section on Eskimo spirituality.

Index

adoptions, 83
akutag ("Eskimo ice cream"), 65
Alaska, 94
    basketball in, 73–75
    military use of, 47
    tourism in, 91, 92, 93
    Yupiks of, 6, 41, 68, 83–84
Alaska Native Land Claim
    Settlement Act
    (ANLCSA), 89–91
alcohol
    alcoholism, 9, 83–87
    introduced by whalers,
      40–41
Alexander, Bryan and Cherry,
    66, 96
animals, 93, 94–95
    hunting, 12, 44–46, 49
    uses of, 16–17, 21–22
atiq (special name), 33–34

basketball, 72–73, 74–75
Beaulieu, Carole, 10
"Between Hunting and Hard
    Rock" (Beaulieu), 10
birds, 94–95
    uses of, 7, 21
Bladder Festival, 49
blubber, 15, 67
Boden, Jergen and Elke, 27
bow drills, 16
breathing holes, seal hunting
    at, 18–19, 46, 66
Brody, Hugh
    on choice of cultures, 88
    on reluctance to understand
      Eskimos, 8
    on structure of Inuktitut
      language, 74
Burch, Ernest S., Jr.
    on dancing, 35

    on Eskimo hatred of
      mosquitoes, 17
    on hunting seals, 43
    on snow houses, 14
butchering, seals, 20, 67

Canada, 6, 47, 83–84, 91, 94
    government support for
      Eskimos, 56–57, 58, 63,
      95–96
    Inuits in, 62, 66
    schooling for Eskimos, 55, 64
Canada North of Sixty
    (Boden), 27
caribou
    dwindling herds of, 56–57,
      61
    uses of, 16, 21, 65
CB radios, 69
celebrations, 34, 70–72
    Bladder Festival, 49
    for suicides, 31
    seal parties, 68–70
ceremonies, marriage, 32
charms, of shamans, 50–51
children
    food for, 32, 63–64
    language problems of, 78–79
    raised lovingly, 32–34
    teen pregnancies, 82–83
    traditions and, 34, 65–66, 87
    see also education; young
      people
cleanliness, 60
    lack of, 51, 77
climate, arctic, 7
    building houses in, 14, 58–59
    effect on vehicles, 58, 62, 74
clothing, 19, 20–22, 33, 46
Coles, Robert and Jane
    Hallowell, 52

communication
    body language, 78
    CB radios, 69
community
    integrating children into, 34
    need for, 26, 47, 66, 70
    protecting, 29–31
    vs. individualism, 27–28, 97
"country foods," 65
culture, 11–12, 26–27, 29–30
    choice of, 88
    influence of outsiders on,
      9–10, 45, 55, 60–61
    traditional
      loss of, 76, 97
      passing on, 34–37, 65–66
      return to, 95–96, 98–99
    values of Eskimo, 27–29, 52,
      84–85, 88

dancing, 35
    drum dancing, 36, 72
    exchange dance, 71
deaths
    alcohol-related, 84
    of infants, 30–31, 32
    suicides, 31
diseases, 16, 41, 64
    alcoholism, 83–87
dogs
    baptism of, 54
    care of, 17, 67
    uses of, 18, 23–25, 61–62
drug use, 9
    see also alcohol
drum dancing, 36, 72

economics
    costs, 62, 63, 95
    housing, 59, 77

income, 57, 68, 92
  of fur trade, 43–44, 46–47
  of land use, 89–91
  of tourism, 91–92
  of whaling, 39–40, 42–43
  subsistence, 12
    decline of Eskimo, 46, 57, 63
  see also jobs
education
  by missionaries, 53, 54–55
  government schools, 55–56
  lack of jobs after, 81–82
  problems in, 76–81
  see also children, traditions and
elders, 31, 76–77
  traditions of, 37, 72
Elizabeth I (queen of England), 38
environment, damage to, 93–95
Eskimo Essays (Fienup-Riordan), 49
Eskimos
  outsiders' distaste for, 39, 50–53
  self-esteem of, 87
The Eskimos (Burch),
  on dancing, 35
  on hunting seals, 43
  on igloo building, 14
Eskimos: Growing Up in a Changing Culture (Meyer), 69
Europeans, 8
  early encounters with, 38–41
  in fur trade, 43–46
exchange dance, 71
exploitation, of Arctic, 43, 46–47, 48

families, 8, 26–27, 30–31, 41, 84
  children in, 32–33, 82–83
  educational problems and, 76–78, 79
  marriages, 31–32, 85-86
Far North
  beauty of, 21
  climate of, 7
  tourism to, 91–93
feathers, in clothing, 21
Fienup-Riordan, Ann
  on exchange dance, 71
  on spirits of seals, 49
fires, 15–16, 17
fish
  fishing, 67
  poisoned by oil spills, 94–95
  sport fishing, 91–93
Fitzhugh, William W., ed., *See Inua: Spirit World of the Bering Sea Eskimo*
food
  changes in, 9, 43, 45–46, 63–64
  cost of, 63
  "country foods," 65
  eating habits, 39
  for dogs, 24–25, 67
  sharing of, 28–29, 68–70
  traditional, 12, 20, 32, 67
The Fourth World: The Heritage of the Arctic and Its Destruction (Hall), military in the Arctic, 58
fox
  fur for clothing, 21
  trade in furs, 44, 45
Frobisher, Martin, 38
furs
  clothing from, 21–22
  European trade in, 43–46

games, 34, 35, 70, 71–72
  basketball, 72–73, 74–75
governments
  support of Eskimos, 55–56, 57, 58, 95–96
  tribal councils and, 73, 89–91
  within bands, 27
ground squirrel, fur for clothing, 21
gussak foods, 63–64
gyms, basketball, 75

Hall, Sam
  description of seal hunters, 19
  on military in the Arctic, 58
  on missionaries to Eskimos, 53
health care, 41, 57
heat
  from lamps, 15–16, 17
  in Eskimo homes, 7, 14, 59
hides, for tents, 16–17
homes, 35
  modern, 57–60, 77
  traditional, 7, 12–15, 16–17, 39, 67
Houston, James
  on hunger, 12
  on language, 78
  on responses to bad behavior, 28
  on sharing of food, 28
humor, teasing as response to bad behavior, 29, 30
hunger. *See* starvation
"Hunters of the Lost Spirit" (Vesilind), 95
hunting, 7, 12, 23, 27
  animals' spirits and, 49
  by outsiders, 42–43, 91–93
  changes in, 9, 44–46, 61
  importance of, 17–18, 65–66, 85–86
  seals, 18–19, 43, 68–70
  sharing meat, 28–29, 97
  territories, 12–13
hypothermia, danger of, 21

ice, 13, 18–19
    sea lanes through, 94
igloos, 13–15, 32, 57–60
individualism, discouragement
    of, 27–28
Inua: Spirit World of the
    Bering Sea Eskimo
    (Nelson), 21, 23
Inuits, 38–39, 67
    economics of, 66, 85, 92, 96
    white culture and, 62, 87
Inupiat, 65, 67, 78

Jenness, Aylette, 11
jobs, 90
    lack of, 46–47, 57, 81
    traditional, 15–16, 18, 22,
        34, 67
junkyards, 58, 62

Kaplan, Susan A., ed., See
    Inua: Spirit World of
    the Bering Sea Eskimo
kayaks, 9, 31
kidnapping, of Eskimos, 38, 41
Kizzia, Tom, 93

lamps, seal oil, 15–16, 17
land, 6–7, 28, 89–91
landscape, of Far North, 21
language, 80–81
    Eskimo, 37, 74, 78–79
    for Eskimo concepts, 27–28
    problems caused by
        English, 54, 55, 76–77,
        78–80
leadership, of Eskimo bands,
    27
lice, 51
light, seal oil lamps, 15–16
Living Arctic: Hunters of the
    Canadian North
    (Brody), 8, 74, 88

maps, 6, 39
marriages, 31–32
    changing roles in, 85–86
men, 68–70, 71
    alcoholism of, 84, 85–86
    jobs of, 15, 18, 85–86
Meyer, Carolyn, 69
migrations, 12, 13, 16–17, 26,
    56
    ending, 57, 63
mining industry, 47, 93–94
mink
    for clothing, 21
    trade in, 44
missionaries, 48
    accommodation of Eskimo
        beliefs, 53–54
    attempts to change
        Eskimos, 50–53, 72
    schools, 54–55
mosquitoes, 17
motorboats, 9, 95
murders
    alcohol-related, 84–85
    to protect community,
        30–31

names
    atiq, 33–34
    Eskimo, 8
Native Americans, 7–8
Nelson, Edward William
    on beauty of Far North, 21
    on sled dogs, 23
    on storyknives, 37
noise
    of missionaries, 52
    during seal hunting, 19
nutritional deficiencies, 64

oil
    seal, 7, 15, 17, 65
    walrus, 42
    whale, 7, 40

oil industry, 47, 57
    environmental damage
        from, 93–95
    tribal councils and, 73, 89–90
Outpost Camp Program, 95–96
outsiders, 80
    arrival of, 38–41, 47
    Eskimo insulation from,
        7–8, 11
    Eskimos' feeling toward,
        87–88, 91–93
    fur trade, 43–46
    missionaries, 48, 50–54
    whalers, 39–43
ownership, concept of, 13, 40,
    91

Pelly, David F., 85
permafrost, building on, 58–59
perspiration, and danger of
    hypothermia, 21
polar bears
    fur for clothing, 21
    trade in furs, 44
population, Eskimo, 7
    growth of, 10, 82–83
poverty, of Eskimo villages,
    56–57, 73–74, 82–83
punishment
    by missionaries, 53, 54
    in Eskimo communities,
        29–30, 33–34, 86

recreation, 60–61, 70–72
    basketball, 72–73, 74–75
    dancing, 35, 36
    games, 34, 35
    singing, 36–37
    storytelling, 37
religion
    traditional Eskimo, 33–34,
        49–51, 53
    see also missionaries
rifles, 44–45, 66

schools, basketball in, 72–73, 74–75
seals
  furs, 44, 66
  hunting, 18–19, 43, 93
  oil, 7, 17, 65
  spirits of, 49
  uses of, 15, 16, 20
self-esteem, of Eskimos, 9–10, 87
shamans, 49–51, 72
sleds, dog, 23–25, 61–62
smallpox, 41
snowmobiles, 6, 9, 61–62, 95
soapstone lamps, 15–16
Social Security, 57
sod igloos, 13–15
  criticism of, 32, 39, 57–58
spirits
  atiq (special names), 33–34
  Eskimo beliefs about, 49, 52
starvation, 12, 30–31
  causes of, 43, 44–46, 56–57
status, 23
  of good hunters, 27, 28
  "stinky heads" (fish heads), 65
storyknives, 37
storytelling, 37, 76–77
subsistence economy, 12
  decline of Eskimo, 46, 57, 63
suicides, of elderly, 31
Sundown, Mary Ann, 13
survival
  Eskimo traditions and, 11–12, 26, 27–28
  necessity of hunting to, 17–18, 41

teachers, 56
teeth
  decay, 64
  worn by chewing leather, 22
television, 6, 80
  impact of, 9–10, 60–61
temperatures, 7, 14, 74
tents, 16–17
territory, of Eskimos, 12–13
tobacco use, 40–41, 69
toilets
  in modern houses, 60
  training, 33
tools, 16, 21, 44–46
  ulu (women's knife), 20, 34
tourism, 91–93
toys, 34
trade
  fur, 44–46
  with whalers, 40
traditions. See culture
transportation
  dogsleds, 23–25, 61–62
  for basketball games, 73, 74
  of food, 63
  of housing materials, 59, 60
traps, 44–45
tribal councils, 73
tuberculosis, 41
tusks, walrus, 42

ulu (women's knife), 20, 34
United States, 66
  support for Eskimos, 55, 56–57, 58, 63, 64

Vesilind, Priit
  on drum dancing, 72
  on Eskimos returning to Alaska, 95
village English, 78–79, 80

villages, 86, 90–91, 95
  changes in, 8–10
  poverty of, 56–57, 73–74, 82–83
violence, alcohol-related, 83–85

Wake of the Unseen Object: Among the Native Cultures of Bush Alaska (Kizzia), 93
walruses, 42–43, 56–57
warmth, maintaining, 14, 20–22
wars, 7–8
welfare, 57
whales, 7, 46
  whaling industry, 39–43
women, 30–31
  jobs of, 15, 18, 20, 22, 67, 85–86
  recreation by, 68–70, 71
Women of Crisis: Lives of Struggle and Hope (Coles), 52

young people
  appreciation for traditions, 97, 98–99
  basketball and, 73, 74–75
  in Eskimo villages, 6, 9–10
  marriage of, 31–32
  problems of, 77–78, 84
  teen pregnancies, 82–83

Yupiks, 6, 78
  diseases among, 41, 84
  economics of, 68, 93
  foods of, 12, 64–65, 67
  missionaries and, 51, 52
  traditions of, 11, 49, 66

Picture Credits

Cover photo: ©Momatiuk/Eastcott/Woodfin Camp & Associates, Inc.

Alaska Stock Images, 70 (bottom)

The Bettmann Archive, 7, 15 (top), 38, 45

Fred Bruemmer, 9, 11, 13, 14, 15 (bottom), 19, 23, 24, 25, 28, 33, 34, 36 (top), 42 (bottom), 48, 56, 57, 59, 60, 61, 63, 64, 69, 70 (top), 72, 80, 81, 89, 90, 91, 92, 94, 96, 97

COMSTOCK/M. Beedell, 62, 65, 78, 79, 87

COMSTOCK/O. Bierwagen, 51

COMSTOCK/G. Hunter, 53, 76

COMSTOCK/E. Otto, 36 (bottom)

COMSTOCK/H. Armstrong Roberts, 86

Culver Pictures, Inc., 32

David Harvey/National Geographic, 77, 84

Hulton Deutsch Collection Limited, 16, 17, 18, 22 (both), 26, 40 (top), 42 (top), 44, 46, 54

©Momatiuk/Eastcott/Woodfin Camp & Associates, Inc., 20, 31, 67, 68, 83, 99

North Wind Picture Archives, 30

Stock Montage, Inc., 39

Damian Strohmeyer/Sports Illustrated, 73, 75

Werner Forman/Art Resource, NY, 40 (bottom), 50 (both)

About the Author

Gail B. Stewart received her undergraduate degree from Gustavus Adolphus College in St. Peter, Minnesota. She did her graduate work in English, linguistics, and curriculum study at the College of St. Thomas and the University of Minnesota. Stewart taught English and reading for more than ten years.

She has written over forty-eight books for young people, including a six-part series called *Living Spaces*. She has written several books for Lucent Books including *Drug Trafficking* and *Acid Rain*.

Stewart and her husband live in Minneapolis with their three sons, two dogs, and a cat. She enjoys reading (especially children's books) and playing tennis.

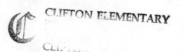